The Elevation
of the
Femalepreneur

Volume 1

Cover Photo of Rebecca Ingram by Tammie Louise
Photography
Cover Photo of Clare Reynolds by Bry Penney
Cover Photo of Di Carter by Keisuke Ohtani
Cover Photo of Emma Hammond by Bori Bojthe
Cover Photo of Chanelle Fry by Chelsa Christensen
Cover Photo of Brandie Thomas by Cara Wagner, Miss
Cara Photography

Typeset by Fuzzy Flamingo
www.fuzzyflamingo.co.uk

Contents

THE VICTORIOUS WOMAN
Brandie Thomas

This chapter is for the woman out there who has lost her identity, lost her self-worth, and lost her purpose. You are worthy of a life of abundance and victory. You are the victorious woman.

This chapter is dedicated to my husband, Jeremy Thomas, who has always encouraged and held space for me to rise as an entrepreneur. Thank you for empowering me to step into my purpose and vision and never holding me back. I love you!

This chapter is dedicated to my mom and dad, Tammy and Lindy Unger, and my sister, Natalie Lawson, who have taught me what it means to live in my truth and my faith. Thank you for your love and guidance throughout my life and helping to form the woman I am today.

Have you ever chased something for so long only to find out once you caught what you were chasing it was not really for you? I realised that, instead of chasing God, I was chasing earthly fame and glory. I could no longer go on suffocating under the noise and chaos that I was allowing this world to bring to my life. I had to make it all stop. I had to find my voice and His voice again. It was not going to be in the parties, businesses, promotions and accolades, or in seeking the approval of others. It was going to be found in the stillness, the whispers. Removing the masks and stripping away everything, I finally found myself again.

My name is Brandie Thomas. I am a woman of faith, a law enforcement officer's wife and grieving infertility, while simultaneously expecting to adopt a newborn child that did not come from me. I am a network marketer and a business and life coach for women of faith in Network Marketing. Like you, I am doing the best I can to show up, love God, love myself and love people. I am learning as I go while helping the woman behind me to not fall into the traps that I did.

This chapter is for the woman out there who has lost her identity, lost her self-worth and purpose. It's for the woman of faith entrepreneur who is seeking to align her business with her divine identity and live in purpose and passion. To do that you will have to be in the world and not of the world. I can tell you that leaning into His purpose and will for your life instead of the unreachable expectations and demands of this world will leave you feeling filled with peace, abundance, love and joy that cannot be explained. I will be sharing how aligning my business with faith-based principles, placing my identity in what God says about me, and speaking my authentic truth brought fulfillment and purpose to my life when I felt like I was suffocating from trying to live up to the world's expectations of me.

I hope by the end of this chapter you are closer to shining your light in the world and have a little more confidence to go left when everyone else is going right. I pray that you will build a purpose-filled business in alignment with your core values. I pray that you feel empowered, inspired and have Holy Spirit confidence to become a fearless influencer in the business world from reading my chapter.

Last year was one of the best years and one of the worst years of my adult life. It was filled with amazing successes and amazing moments, but I also hit rock bottom. I have been involved in the network marketing industry for the past ten years. In the last five years, I found a company that I could really put my name to, and I had built a business that brought me success. It brought many blessings to my family's life and for that I will be forever grateful. It introduced me to personal development, dreaming big, and believing in myself. Unfortunately, it also introduced me to imposter syndrome, comparison, and putting my self-worth in achieving the next rank and promotion.

I was chasing the approval of others and trying to live up to expectations that were not in alignment with my core values. Can you relate to this? If so, I'd love for you to read on as I share some important lessons that I have learned throughout my journey. I hope it may inspire you to find the strength and light that I did.

So, lesson number one is identifying your core values. According to Yourdictionary.com, "Core values are the fundamental beliefs of a person or organisation. These guiding principles dictate behaviour and can help people… fulfill their goals by creating an unwavering guide."

Looking back, I realise I had compromised for so long, giving up time with friends, time with God, and even time healing myself to achieve a certain rank within my company. When I earned that rank and even got to share about it on stage at our national conference, it was one of the highest moments of my network marketing career. So, why then did it feel so empty? Why did I feel so hollow?

After months of pushing, striving and camouflaging my truth with the next project, or next event, I finally hit rock bottom, crying on the bathroom floor. Sitting alone with myself, I realised I had not earned my success in a way that was in alignment with my highest self. I reached the top and turned around to see more destruction in my path than growth. I was tired, burnt out and wondering if everything I sacrificed was worth the expense. Instead of feeling joy and excitement, I was apathetic and unimpressed. I needed to get back in alignment.

Before aligning to my core values, I had to figure out who I was, what I wanted for my life, and what God wanted for my life. Micah 6:8 says that the Lord requires you to "act justly and to love mercy and to walk humbly with your God." With this in mind, I identified the areas of my life that I cared about. The areas that I wanted to see thrive.

My core values are to be spiritually, mentally, physically, relationally and financially healthy. Once

I realigned with my core values, I began to see my fulfillment and passion come back to my life and business. Below are my core values and how I set specific ways I could live them out in my daily life.

1. Spending time with God daily – devotional, prayer journal, or listen to sermon.
2. Self-Care/Health – exercising three times per week, meditation, reading and time blocking rest.
3. Quality time with loved ones.
4. Organised space – cleaning or tidying up once a week.
5. Finances – pay off debt, monthly deposits for savings and tithe.

I believe that you can build a successful business while living in alignment with your core values. You do not have to be on everyone else's timeline and you do not have to get success the same way as others. We were meant to "throw off everything that hinders and entangles us and run with perseverance the race marked out for us", as Paul writes to us in Hebrews 12:1. I believe that your life and business are a beautiful symphony being orchestrated. Do not be afraid to let it play out and be you.

In this world and in business, we can lose ourselves and lose our voice. So, lesson two is stand in your identity as a daughter of God. Sister, you are royalty! If you do not believe me, then read the truth for yourself. Only His words can define who you are, and I like His definition.

1. "Before I formed you in the womb, I knew you, before you were born, I set you apart; I appointed you as a prophet to the nations." – Jeremiah 1:5
2. "But you are a chosen people, a royal priesthood, a holy nation, God's special possession, that you may declare the praises of him who called you out of darkness into his wonderful light." – 1 Peter 2:9
3. "See what great love the Father has lavished on us, that we should be called children of God! And that is what we are!" – 1 John 3:1
4. "I am God's handiwork created in Christ Jesus to do good works which was prepared in advance for me to do." – Ephesians 2:10
5. "And even the very hairs on your head are all numbered. So, don't be afraid; you are worth more than many sparrows." – Matthew 10:30-31

What a disservice we bring the world and a dishonour we bring to Him when we do not stand in our truth. We were not created to show up in this world as a copy and paste social media post. You have a unique identity that gives you a unique story. Share it! Stand in it! Trust me, when you can be vulnerable with others and let your light shine, you will attract others to you who need the warmth from your glow.

I learned this when I forgot who I am and whose I am. I searched for approval, love and companionship from those who did not have my best interest at heart. I behaved in ways that I am now ashamed of and that were uncharacteristic of who I am called to be as a daughter of God. I totally lost myself. I was searching for my identity in social media posts, in unhealthy relationships, and unrealistic expectations. Fortunately, I do have people in my life who genuinely care about me and reminded me of who I am. They told me what I am about to tell you: Your past failures and mistakes do not define you or your future. Stop standing in them. They are not serving you or this world. This world needs you and what you have to offer.

So, sister, lesson three is to remind you that you have the power within to rise and be successful. It is your birthright to live in victory and abundance. Take captive of your negative thoughts and fears that are telling you that you are unworthy, not enough, will never measure up or whatever lies your inner mean girl is telling you. You were not given a "spirit of fear, but a spirit of power, love, and self-discipline" to be successful, as 2 Timothy 1:7 reminds us. Take those limiting beliefs that may be swirling in your brain causing mind drama and flip them into positive affirmations. Speak life and truth, not lies.

One of the best ways to take captive of your mind drama is to become aware of what stories you are telling yourself. I have found that writing my thoughts down allows me to truly see how I am speaking to myself. I can sort out the lies of my inner voice and begin the practice of flipping my inner dialogue and reprogramming my mind to speak truth. Doing this practice will allow you to gain clarity on where these thoughts and stories are coming from in your subconscious. Are these stories or thoughts from an insecurity? Are they from what someone told you years ago that you have held onto and chose to wear as a piece of your identity? Are they from a perception that you created based on someone's reaction? The more clarity you can gain around the root cause of your beliefs, the easier it will be for you to remove the toxic thinking that is holding you back from achieving the potential *and* beauty in store for you in your life and business.

When I was knee deep in my mind drama, I was telling myself that "I am not a good leader", "I am not worthy of good things because of my mistakes" and, worst of all, "I am a failure". Honestly, writing this story out for you just now still invokes emotions of sadness for allowing myself to say such awful and hurtful things to myself. I love the saying, "You would not talk to your best friend like that so why would you talk to yourself with so much hate?" There is so much truth to this statement. It is so sad that we can be so quick to help a friend and build them up when they are going through a difficult time, but we are the first to cut ourselves down, judge ourselves, and blame ourselves for not living up to whatever crazy expectation we or someone else has put on ourselves. It is truly heartbreaking when you realise how mean you actually are to yourself.

Reprogramming your mind so that your inner nice girl is louder than your inner mean girl is a daily practice. Once you have identified the stories and beliefs that are not supporting the vision and future you want to step into, then you can start speaking truth over your life. I love using the acronym F+GOAT to prompt and lead me in this practice twice a day:

F   stands for Forgiveness. Forgive yourself of your mistakes, your beliefs, your shame, whatever may be coming up for you today.

G   stands for Gratitude. Come to a place of gratitude and say or think of what in your life you are truly grateful for.

O   stands for Oxygen. Take deep breaths. Oxygen is so good for your body and your soul. Breathe in love and exhale gratitude.

A   stands for Affirmation. Take one or more of your limiting beliefs and rewrite them into a positive affirmation. Speak these at least two times a day out loud.

T   stands for Truth. I love supporting my positive affirmation with a Bible verse. For example, if my affirmation is that *I am strong*, then my Bible verse might be Philippians 4:13, "I can do all things through Christ who strengthens me".

I have found practicing F+GOAT in the shower is a great place for this daily practice. I like to picture the negativity washing off me and visualise love pouring onto me. Try it! I pray that you feel God's love, grace, mercy and forgiveness wash over you as you allow yourself to let go and stand empowered.

As this chapter comes to an end, I hope you can take these three lessons and implement them into your life. I pray you can shorten the learning curve and find your truth and voice more quickly than I did. You have a calling to show up, love yourself, and love people. I believe that you have been put in the business world to do just that in your own unique way. Do not conform to the expectations of the world and do not compare your journey to someone else's. You are made for such a time as this and are exactly where you are supposed to be. Stand in the truth that you are loved and have Holy Spirit empowerment to be a fearless influencer and bless this world with your light. Listen to your voice. Listen to His voice. Use those as your guiding lights and allow them to direct you into your calling. You can make an impact in this world and in His Kingdom.

You are worthy of a life of abundance and victory. Rise up and live your purpose.

★★★

Brandie, who lives in Indianapolis, IN, has been described as an inspiring woman of faith who serves and leads with her heart. She enjoys her network marketing business and mentoring other women of faith in the industry with her business and mindset coaching program. Family is very important to Brandie, and she enjoys spending quality time with her son and husband.

Brandie is passionate about helping other women

live a life designed in alignment with their core values and serve the community around them. She truly believes we all were put here to live a victorious life and can serve our purpose by showing up, loving ourselves, and loving people.

You can find Brandie here:

www.instagram.com/livevictorious

https://linktr.ee/livevictorious

LADIES, YOU DESERVE YOUR DREAMS

Rebecca Ingram

This book is dedicated to my children and my mum. Firstly, to my daughter, Bibi. Her arrival into my world was the catalyst for my healing journey, she empowered me and woke me. How lucky I am to have my very own live-in lightworker. Secondly, to my son, Rocco, who has taught me more about the beauty of the male soul than I ever thought possible, thank you for choosing me. Finally, to my mum, my best friend, my rock. Without your never-ending support I wouldn't have been able to do any of the things that make me, me. You are all amazing, and I am so grateful to have you in my life.

On my knees, wet, tear-streaked face on the cold, hard floor, darkness and silence all around me. An empty, churning, desperate ache, deep in my soul. I heard a raw, guttural sound leave me: "Please help me, Universe, I can't do this any more."

I stayed there for a little while, as all the things I had been through were running through my mind… childhood abuse, bullying, narcissistic abuse, violence, the utter devastation of having decided to break up my children's family home because deep down I knew it wasn't healthy, then solo pregnancy and single motherhood with a poorly little boy who couldn't sleep longer than two hours at a time, while also juggling a corporate career and building a business on the side.

I was through the worst of all of this, but still I wasn't seeing the success I wanted in my business. When I first became a single mum I was a lawyer in a corporate firm with a three-hour round commute. Later, I worked for a local firm so had lost the long commute (and taken a huge pay drop) and yet still never seemed to have enough time to build my network marketing business. Every night I'd get home at seven o'clock, put the kids to bed, sit at my laptop and go to work; every single night. I was frustrated, bored, exhausted and ready to quit on my dreams. I was so tired of seeing no consistent business income; I would have a good month, then poor, up and down, feast and famine. I was done. I was never going to be able to leave my corporate career at this rate.

I'd trained as a yoga teacher while on maternity leave but had struggled to get a successful class going as I didn't have the funds to pay for a reputable babysitter and I hated relying on family all the time – asking for help was not my strong point.

So, here I was – big firm lawyer and I couldn't even get a consistent yoga class going, never mind build a six-figure business. I had tried to enjoy my job, I really, really had. I mean the salary was okay, it had status, but day after day I would sit, trying desperately to focus on the boring paragraphs in front of me. All the while, underneath the yellow strip lights of the office, staring out of the locked windows at the city lights, feeling more and more trapped and panicky and like life was just passing me by. I missed my children, I missed fresh air. Always rushing from nursery drop-off to station, to work, and back again – always panicking that I was going to be late, or drop one of the many balls I was juggling. I looked around the office and saw some of the cleverest minds around me, but all feeling the same as me. No one was happy, no one smiled, no one even talked to each other. It was depressing and I was depressed.

Even though I'd had a very loving mum and sisters around me as a child, I was the only one in our family with drive – so no one really understood my yearning to achieve more, be more and do more. I had that fire inside that never really goes away for longer than a few hours. So, no one had ever really expected much of me because they didn't expect much of themselves in the way of business success, either. I desperately yearned for someone to expect more of me. Even as an A-grade student I was laughed at when, in my careers meeting, I said I wanted to be a managing director. I was told I should be a hairdresser. In fact, everyone laughed at me my whole life when I said I wanted to be a managing director. Not a single person encouraged me, or guided me, or even told me I could do it. No one expected anything from me, maybe because I was blonde and blue-eyed. As the daughter of a sexually-abusive man, who objectified women daily, even I had never questioned that my role wasn't to just look pretty, but it definitely made me angry.

I'd spent many years judging myself solely on my looks, comparing myself to others and, while I knew I could achieve great things intellectually, I didn't believe it in my heart. I had such unhealthy boundaries I let people take and take until I was burnt out. I was the ultimate people-pleaser, taking care of everyone else before me. Putting myself last all the time, unable to relax, unable to say no. I would have loved to have had someone, anyone, who could see past the blonde hair and see the bright, intelligent girl with the fire in her soul. Maybe if I'd had this, it wouldn't have taken me so long to get to where I am now. Maybe if I'd have listened to the schoolteacher who asked me not to leave school at fifteen because of the bullies, but to stay on and do my A-levels, then maybe it wouldn't have been such a circuitous route to fulfillment.

After school, I had a number of jobs – modelling, sales and recruitment – until I decided to go to university and train as a psychologist. I worked almost full-time while studying and still came out with a first. I loved it. Because of my aptitude, I was fast-tracked straight onto a funded PhD. I threw my heart and soul into my studies, but the funding was pulled after a year due to complications outside of my control. I was devastated. Even though I was offered another PhD, I felt depleted and didn't want to commit in case the same thing happened again. I decided to apply to a law firm for a "vacation" scheme. I was accepted and ultimately offered a training contract with a top-ten law firm. I was thrilled, but at the same time, deep down, I knew it wasn't for me – my soul was definitely not fulfilled. But, I was in it now. I trudged on.

Fast forward ten years, I was exhausted and drained. My confidence was at rock-bottom, I just did not believe that I could carry on juggling a soul-destroying corporate career while also trying to build a business. I needed help and even yoga – the thing that got me through my divorce – was not helping me. I had come such a long way from being the very broken woman that had walked away from her marriage, but I was still battling chronic sleep deprivation, PTSD and overwhelming feelings of hopelessness, as well as the awful anxious feelings of being trapped, not only by my circumstances, but also by me. Deep down, I knew it was me that was holding me back – all the excuses in the world about tiredness, lack of time and so on, were exactly that – just excuses. If other women could make a success of their businesses while also working and being single mums, why couldn't I make it work?! I felt stuck, like there was a HUGE me waiting to get out but something in me was blocking it. As hard as I tried, doing all the usual affirmations, vision boards, journaling, etc., I just could NOT get over what was blocking me and do the things I needed to do. I was so frustrated with myself I wanted to tear my hair out.

I yearned to have a life of freedom, to be there for my children when they needed me. I wanted a significant, consistent, reliable income so that I could travel, be with my babies, give them the experiences I never had. I wanted to have time for me; to breathe, to read, to spend time in nature, to relax. I wanted to create a legacy that fulfilled me and made me proud

I needed clarity, I needed focus, I needed something really powerful and I needed it now.

So, here I am on my knees in the darkness begging the Universe for help. Over the next week, six people mentioned RTT to me. RTT is Rapid Transformational Therapy and I saw this as a sign, so I looked for a local RTT therapist. The next morning I spoke to a lady who, the night before, had written out a description of her "ideal client": 'stressed out corporate mum looking to make the leap'. So, I saw it as another sign and signed up immediately to book a package with her.

This was the beginning of the change. My first RTT session was so powerful, my t-shirt was drenched from the huge release of tears. We addressed all my underlying feelings of not being good enough, not being worthy and feeling undeserving of success. Almost immediately, I noticed a shift, I found myself leaning into things I would have usually shied away from. Opportunities started to miraculously appear from nowhere and my confidence was rock solid. I was able to recognise my strengths and how best I could utilise them. And, when we worked on my money blocks, wow! RTT is like manifesting on steroids, and I could feel it working for me.

One of the biggest things that has got me to where I am now is learning what healthy boundaries are, and implementing strategies to maintain them. With the help of RTT, this was almost instant and, as I healed, toxic people either fell away, or it appeared that they healed too – it was incredible to watch. Another key factor in my journey was regaining my sleep. Was it also a coincidence that at the same time I found a natural product that helped my little boy's body heal naturally? With this support, my boy started sleeping – finally. After three and a half years of chronic sleep deprivation, hallucinations, emotional distress and hair loss, I started to feel human again.

I knew what I had to do.

I had to train as an RTT Therapist so I could give the gift of this powerful, life-changing tool to others.

Now I can offer RTT combined with proven executive coaching strategies and my unique blend of ancient yogic science to help transform the lives and businesses of other women.

I know that all the strategies in the world will get you nowhere if you haven't done the deep inner work that is holding you back. I can honestly say I have never felt better. I have left the corporate world and I spend my days working with incredible entrepreneurs and professionals who are ready to create massive transformation and success in their lives. I feel grounded and confident; I attract amazing people and opportunities to me all of the time.

If I had to pick a single thing that has helped me go from stressed-out corporate mum crying on my knees to empowered entrepreneur, it would be RTT. As a highly spiritual person anyway, I didn't think my vibe could have been raised any higher. How wrong was I? The reason RTT is so powerful is because it literally erases the bad thoughts and feelings you have, and replaces them with positive ones that will help you achieve your goals.

With my exclusive method, you become so aligned to your desires, the Universe has to deliver you your dreams. I have seen it in myself, and I now see it over and over again in my clients. Women who, like me, have had enough of accepting what life has given them and who are prepared to clear all the stuff that is holding them back, in order to connect to their deepest values and create lives in alignment with them.

If this sounds like you, I want you to know this, from the bottom of my heart and with every single cell, you have got this. You are not your past and you can release yourself. The things you believe to be true, the stories you tell yourself, are not you and you can rewrite them. Your habits, thoughts and behaviours are not you and you can rewire them in a new way to create a new life. Slow down, take a breath, your dreams won't stop coming if you take a rest. Put yourself first, learn where you need to put boundaries in place and do so. Say no. Stop being the goddamn good girl and be the woman you really are. Step into the depths of your deep, dark side and embrace that. Stop letting yourself down, you are a queen and you deserve the best. Stop compromising, stop playing small, stop dimming your light just to make others feel brighter. You are loveable, you are worthy of everything you desire, you are good enough and you are needed. The world needs your light, your power and your service. Your dreams need you. Your time is now.

You can rise from the ashes and create a life brighter than you ever thought possible. I know, because I have done it. Slow down, connect to you, work out a plan and keep going. I believe in you from the centre of my core. Vibe so high the negative people slip from your life and, if they don't, you will learn to stop listening to them because what they say will matter less. Make your vision so real, so powerful, so tangible you can actually feel what it is like to live your dream.

I believe in you, and so must you.

It is hard to believe I was ever the person I used to be. RTT completely changes the way we feel at a deep soul level and it is hard to remember how I used to feel. But, as I wrote this chapter and dipped into old diaries and journals, the memories resurfaced, and I felt sad for the wounded woman I once was. It's funny, when you are going through bad times, you just get on with it, but when you look back, with greater awareness, you can see how bad things were. I can feel that desperation of wanting to be seen for the real me, and I wonder why no one else could see this. Would I have changed anything? Maybe a few things but, in the main, no. With all my experiences and challenges, I have such a depth to draw on to help my clients. I understand the lows, the desperation.

I have truly walked the walk from survivor to thriver and I help my clients to face their internal battles and create massive transformation in a way that makes their soul soar. I am so excited for the future and what it holds for us all. The joy of running a business that lights you up and that gives you the freedom to spend with your loved ones. The security of a consistent, significant income so you have peace of mind and fulfillment from knowing that you are creating a wonderful legacy for your loved ones.

★★★

Rebecca is an experienced Rapid Transformational Therapist, Coach, Author and Yoga Teacher. She is the creator of Success Activator Quadrant, which she uses to facilitate profound inner transformation and success in her clients. Rebecca has been featured on various radio programmes and podcasts.

Rebecca works with ambitious women all over the world who are ready to step fully into their powerful feminine energy to create their vision of success in life, business and career.

She is intuitive, heart-led and when not working with amazing clients she solo parents two young children. She loves yoga, meditation, nature and red wine.

You can find Rebecca here:

www.rebeccaingram.co.uk
www.facebook.com/rebeccaingramcoach
https://www.instagram.com/rapid_transformation_coach/

Hopelessness
to Empowerment

Samantha Jane

*I dedicate this chapter to my husband and boys who give me the
motivation to be the best version of myself every day.*

Welcome to my chapter. I'm Sam: speaker, author and
change maker. I am passionate about helping people to
create consistency and cultivate positive habits within
their lives and businesses.

I am the CEO of two companies and the creator of
The Habits of Happiness, which has been delivered within
schools, colleges and corporate and is at the core of my
coaching programmes.

We have to back up ten years to find out how I arrived
here.

How did I come from a place of hopelessness to a place of empowerment?

Ten years ago, I ran my own business as a make-up artist
specialising in wedding hair and make-up all over Scotland.

It had really grown from strength to strength over the past three years. I absolutely loved what I did, being my own boss, as well as being part of someone's big day. I had an amazing team of freelance stylists that worked with me. I was booked up to a year in advance. I was doing a wedding every weekend, sometimes two in one day. In my mind, I was doing great, earning an income through what I loved. Little did I know that, within twenty-four hours, my whole life would change forever.

JANUARY 3RD, 2010: THE DAY EVERYTHING CHANGED

I woke to find the whole left side of my body completely paralysed. I could not move my arm. I could not move my leg. I knew I had to stay calm for my two sons, who were nine and six at the time, but I was terrified! My husband was at work, so there was no adult in the house to help. I called my eldest to my room and asked him if he could go to my friend Alison's house, who lived just a few doors from us. She came straight over and called the ambulance, and I will always be eternally grateful for her help. They rushed me into the hospital and carried out numerous tests to try to find out what caused my paralysis. I was eventually transferred to the neurology department for further tests. After weeks of tests and nothing definite showing up, they finally told me that it was psychosomatic (which in layman's terms means stress had brought on the symptoms and they could not find any other cause). It took four months for the power to come back fully into the left side of my body. I was left with nerve pain and weakness down the left side and, when I was on long journeys, the symptoms would become worse. For years they looked into what was wrong, treating me for fibromyalgia by putting me on numerous nerve-blocking pain drugs and muscle relaxers to help with the pain. I resigned myself to the fact that I would have to slow down and eventually gave up my business in 2013 and went back to part-time freelance work.

This took its toll on my mental health. I felt as if I was on an emotional roller coaster of ups and downs, one moment I was having negative thoughts about it being psychosomatic and feeling powerless about it all, along with feeling I was a hypochondriac. The next moment I would tell myself to get a grip, there was nothing wrong, and I would push myself until I was mentally, physically and emotionally exhausted.

Deep down, I always knew that there had to be more to life than the way I was living. I had never been religious or spiritual, but I had always had awareness and curiosity about the unknown (God, the universe, call it what you wish). Becoming aware and asking for help was my first step, although it did take another three years before I truly started to listen to my inner guidance. This was when my self-discovery journey truly started.

I first got introduced to self-development, mindset and the power of the subconscious mind by joining my first MLM company. It truly opened my eyes to the power that we hold within us. The book *The Secret* introduced me to the idea of The Law of Attraction and, for the first time in years, I felt excited! I was starting to feel in control of my own life again, having this new knowledge of my thoughts creating my reality and the power of mindset and the subconscious; it really gave me the push I needed to start making the changes in my life.

I discovered we are all creating our own reality and future with our thoughts. This concept was hard to grasp at the beginning. I had many beliefs about how it was other people and things that were creating my reality, and I had no power over these things.

Once I realised it was down to me, everything completely shifted for me. From being in a state of victimhood and feeling powerless, to shifting to a place of empowerment. This really gave me the boost I needed to realise that I had more power over my life than I ever knew was possible. However, I soon came to realise that my mind was filled with negative self-talk and fear-based thoughts (I had always thought I was a strong, determined person, which I was on the surface). I was filled with doubt and self-loathing, shame, guilt; with all these thoughts going round in my head, no wonder I was not able to create the life I truly knew I wanted.

The good thing was, I was open, and my mind was learning, and the universe sent with open arms! I was like a sponge and, for the next few years, I learned about the mind-body connection, the power of the subconscious mind, about the flow of the universe, vibrational energy and how we are all made of energy.

I discovered how I could raise my vibration by using different methods. Using powerful positive affirmations helped me retrain my subconscious brain into a more positive way of thinking and, in turn, lifted my vibrational energy.

The more I learned how to retrain my thoughts, the more the universe showed up for me. The more I felt connected, the more I felt the shift in my mind and body, too; less pain, more confidence, less anxiety, and less negative self-talk.

After years of researching so many different areas of well-being, training courses and qualifications, I finally got that aha moment, but not how I expected it to be. There was no great flash of lightning or sign from above.

What I came to realise was: awareness is the key and the connection between it all. When I became aware, I started living in the present moment with acceptance, recognising my thoughts, feelings, sensations, not passing judgment or being critical of those thoughts, feelings, sensations, and not comparing myself to others. I also learned how to shift my awareness to become the observer of my thoughts rather than being attached to them and caught up in the emotion of them.

I also learned that what we think we become, what emotional energy (anger, shame, gratitude, love) we give to something, in turn gives it its power. Whether that is good or bad, the universe/subconscious does not care what we focus our emotional energy on (thoughts and feelings); if that is in lack and the feeling of not enough, the universe/subconscious will send more of that.

Once I started to understand this, it was like a lightbulb went off in my head. The thousands of questions I had wanted to be answered, like how come everyone else manifests their dreams but not me – in whatever area of life, love, work, spiritual or financial?

What I discovered was their beliefs, thoughts, actions and intentions held power. And the reason I was not experiencing days filled with joy and fulfillment, was down to my subconscious mind. Many old, limited and toxic belief systems were hiding out in my subconscious mind and secretly running things.

When I was focusing on my current state of misery, scarcity and 'want', then I received more of the same.

Our beliefs are at the core of what creates our reality. The sad thing is a high percentage of these beliefs are not even ours, they have been instilled in us in childhood and then reinforced as we grow up. What I found out was that whether we believe we can achieve something or whether we believe we cannot is ultimately true for us.

So how do we get past this? I discovered our beliefs are really just habitual thought patterns. Once we learn how to recognise these negative thought patterns and negative self-talk that no longer serve us, we can then use tools such as the power of affirmation, asking the right question, creating a gratitude practice, learning to surrender to the unknown and letting go of control of the outcome to create new positive habits. Letting go of control of the outcome can be one of the hardest things to do as our subconscious brain is designed to solve problems. Trying to figure out every detail, whether it is better health, money, or love, our subconscious is constantly trying to control the outcome and, more often than not, that includes a fear-based outcome.

The key is consistency and building new positive habits, through cultivating self-love and awareness practices, along with recognising our negative thoughts (I am not good enough), emotions (of shame, anger, comparison) and our connection to our body (recognising tension, heart rate). The hardest thing to learn is increasing our awareness without judgment of ourselves. This is still the hardest thing for me – to not judge myself.

I'm no guru, I still have lots of wobbles, but I have now developed a seven-step routine and a toolbox to help me.

If I can do it, you can too, I am not saying it was easy, but it is definitely worth it. You have the power within you to achieve anything. When we start to take our power back, we can start to heal ourselves and the world around us.

This leads me to how I used what I learned to become a coach, speaker, author and change maker.

As I mentioned earlier, I was first introduced to self-development and change work through my MLM company. I had achieved some success within this company, building a team and learning about coaching and growth mindset, and this is when I realised my true passion was in helping other women grow in confidence and become the best version of themselves. I then went on to train in different coaching qualifications: Mind Mediation Therapy, Clinical Hypnotherapy, Mindfulness, The Science of Happiness NLP, and many more. Doing this also contributed to my healing physically, mentally, emotionally and spiritually.

This is when I truly started my research, researching hundreds of different articles from numerous experts in their fields related to the mind-body connection. I wanted to find out the science of what had happened to me ten years ago. But also, what things had I been doing (mainly my seven-step morning routine) that were having such a positive impact on my life. I started to uncover how powerful each step was on their own but, when put together in the seven-step process, this was the key to my change.

In the process of all my learning, I discovered the power of habits. To give you a little understanding: habits are rituals and behaviours that we perform automatically, allowing us to carry out essential activities such as brushing our teeth, taking a shower, getting dressed for work and following the same routes every day without thinking about them. We all have habits, and we activate hundreds every day. I discovered I had developed what were essentially new positive habits that were helping to retrain my brain to become happier. My vibrational energy had been raised, which in turn helped me mentally, physically, emotionally and spiritually, and I seemed to be attracting things to me effortlessly. Don't be mistaken, though, I was still working really hard. Things seemed to be aligning with what my vision was, and opportunities were arising in line with my vision.

It has grown from being just my morning routine to my passion and purpose. It is in every part of my life, from my morning routine to the way I live my life, it is incorporated in everything I do, from my home life to my business. It is the foundation of my coaching programme and the inspiration behind *The Habits of Happiness Coaching*, where I have been lucky enough to be a keynote speaker within colleges, corporate and my local community, courses, online workshops and in person. It is at the core of my one-to-one coaching sessions, helping female entrepreneurs break through their limiting beliefs, gaining clarity and consistency within their life and businesses to it being the foundation of my new social project being incorporated into schools.

You are capable of more than you believe, you have limitless potential within you. Do not let what anyone says, thinks, or does to you disempower who you are. You have the power within you to change your life. Remember, whatever you think is holding you back from your best life, you have the power to change this with the power of your thinking and the actions you take. You are creating your reality every moment, change your thinking – change your reality.

I went from feeling powerless and afraid, mentally, physically, and emotionally at my lowest, and losing my business, to now feeling the strongest I have ever been physically, mentally, emotionally and spiritually. I finally feel I have achieved balance in my life, I have amazing businesses that I love, and I ensure I make time for myself and my family. Now I live life on my terms.

The most powerful thing I have learned through this journey is 'happiness is an inside job'. It may sound such a cliché, but I had been searching for so long outside of myself, I nearly lost sight of my power within me. I am not saying we do not need guidance and others to help, but like a locked treasure chest, once you have the key, you have access to the treasure within any time.

As the late Wayne Dyer said, "Our intention creates our reality." And I said above, "What you think, you become."

That is why intention is the first step in my seven-step process.

Learn more about *The Habits of Happiness* in my new book *My Seven Secrets to Happiness* out on the 7th July 2020.

★★★

Samantha is a therapist, coach, speaker, author and changemaker. She is passionate about helping people to create consistency and cultivate positive habits within their lives and businesses.

She is the CEO of two companies and the creator of The Habits of Happiness, which has been delivered within schools, colleges and is at the core of her coaching programmes.

She lives in Scotland with her amazingly supportive husband, Daren, and their two teenage boys who are her motivation, drive and incentive for her success both financially and mentally.

Her mission is to help as many people as she can reawaken to the power and happiness they already have within themselves.

You can find Samantha here:

www.thehabitsofhappinesscoaching.com
Email: sam@thehabitsofhappinesscoaching.com

No Mud, No Lotus

Maggie Byron

I dedicate this chapter to any woman who feels less than she truly is – your true self is in there, believe in her. And also to the one who saved me, my daughter Lyla – I hope you always know how very special you are, keep your strong heart and mind, baby girl, you'll need it.

7TH MAY 2014

'I used to think that the worst thing in life was to end up all alone. It's not! The worst thing in life is to end up with people who make you feel all alone.'

As I lay with my almost six-month old baby beside me, I felt lost, crushed, exhausted. I felt that unbearable raw pain that only comes with losing someone so close to you. I had spent all night with my mum, trying to keep her comfortable, saying my goodbyes and my thank yous for all she had done and ultimately watching her life slip away.

She had been suffering for years with a debilitating lung condition but also depression and anxiety, so a small part of me almost felt relieved that she was finally at peace, and that she was going to be with my dad who had passed away suddenly three years before. They were inseparable and I watched a part of her die that day she lost her life partner and she was never the same after – and neither was I. Anxiety had started after my dad had passed away as I had realised how quickly life can change in the blink of an eye; anything can be taken away at any moment, nothing is promised and these thoughts affected me daily. Life didn't seem what it once was, it seemed cruel and unfair and uncertain, and I would always have this feeling something awful was going to happen. But everyone had always viewed me as this strong person, so it was difficult for me to talk about how I was feeling to anyone, and now I had to be strong for the people around me, so I tried my best to not show it and just move on with my life.

I tried my best to look like I was strong and keeping it together, but inside I was broken, I felt empty. I wasn't giving myself the time to grieve properly. I ended up in a relationship that I now know was not right for me at all, but at first it felt great; it was like an escape, something to take my mind off everything else. But really and truly we were not compatible and I still wasn't giving myself the time to properly grieve. Shortly after, the relationship turned sour. It was abusive, jealous and toxic, I lost myself completely and, after a while, I had absolutely no self-worth left. People always wonder why people stay in these types of situations and the truth is you don't see it the way people do from the outside when it's happening to you. Little by little, things get worse, but you're losing parts of yourself along the way. I don't think you truly realise until you start to gain your old self back.

I had been called the most disgusting names in jealous fits of rage and I had lost myself so much that I believed it to be true; I felt worthless, and almost ashamed of myself. Around this time, I would sometimes suffer with anxiety attacks going out and socialising, terrified of what would happen, so I eventually stopped going as it was easier that way. And so, I lost touch with lots of my friends and the ones I did speak to were sick of hearing about it and me not leaving, but I was stuck in this cycle of believing things would eventually change and believing all the lies and the apologies. So, I eventually stopped telling anyone anything, almost embarrassed of what I would put up with and so I became more and more isolated and stuck in an existence that just felt lonely.

And then I found out I was pregnant. It was so unexpected and I was shocked but I felt excited. I had never thought about having children before, but this felt like it was meant to be, like it was something that needed to happen and I thought I would make it work for this baby's sake. But the pregnancy was so hard, I spent most of it alone, I found out about multiple affairs and lies and was treated like I didn't even matter. I slipped into a deep depression that I hid from everyone around me. My life seemed such a mess that I didn't even know how to begin talking about it. I was so alone; every day was spent crying and what should have been the best time of my life was filled with worry and anxiety. I tried to hide it and I even saw counsellors to try and get over what I was feeling. I was terrified at the thought of facing life as a single mum, terrified of how I would cope, financially and mentally, and I even worried about what people would think of me.

But then when my little girl came and I looked at her beautiful little face, I knew she needed me and I needed her and no matter what life threw at us, alone or not, I would do everything I could to make sure she had everything she needed in life. She was my constant in the chaos, she was the only certain thing in my whole world and I look back now and I just know that she was sent to me for a reason; she was sent to me because she was my reason to keep going no matter what.

So here I was, twenty-six years old, lost both my parents, my self-worth, my confidence, and struggling financially. But I had this beautiful little girl that I had to make things work for. And so, I went back to work when Lyla was eight months old, as I had to financially, still living in a toxic relationship, still suffering with the loss of both my parents, trying to juggle work, mum life and paying out half of what I earned in childcare and having nothing left at the end of the month. I knew something had to change, I just didn't know how.

Ever since I can remember, I always had that feeling that I was made for more, I always had that feeling that something was missing, that there was more to life than nine-to-fives and financial struggles and mundane routines, surely. I wanted Lyla to be able to enjoy life, I wanted to show her more of the world. There had to be something out there, I just didn't know yet what it was. I looked for opportunities that I could work from home, as there was no way I could afford more childcare and I didn't want to be away from Lyla all of the time.

I tried an online business for a while, but I didn't have much success at all. It felt as if something wasn't right. I know now that it was my mind. I was still telling myself I wasn't good enough because that's all I had ever been told. I was listening to voices around me that were stuck in my head and I was letting doubt creep in. I didn't know how to change it then, and so I gave up on myself.

It was a few years later when I finally found my tribe. I came across a network marketing company that was everything I wanted and something I could really be passionate about. There have been very few times in my life where I have felt absolute certainty about something, but this was one of them. I knew I had to do it. Everything felt right and it was perfect for me. And so, I got involved and made it my mission to learn absolutely everything I could.

I went to events to learn more and, through doing this, I made new friends who were positive, who all had the same focus, and who knew nothing of what had happened before, so it felt easier to be myself again and forget anything else that was going on. This was something for me and it gave me something to focus on, to work towards. It gave me an escape and it gave me hope that the future was brighter.

The thing I love most about network marketing is

how it forces you to level up as a person, how sometimes you don't even realise it, but you are developing a little bit each day and, before you know it, everything has changed. I learned a little more each day and I began to realise I was good at something, that I was getting better, and with the support of the people around me my confidence began to grow. I then learned about self development and how important the right mindset is in business and I put focus into that every single day, growing and developing in any way I could. I began to learn about the Law of Attraction and the power of positivity and gratitude, not just in business, but in life as a whole, and I noticed things beginning to change for me.

The business I loved that had given me a new lease of life and a focus had started to take off. I had multiple promotions, some amazing trips, made solid friendships, I was beginning to earn a good income and could enjoy the little extras in life that I never could before. The late nights and early mornings were paying off and I was overwhelmed and so, so proud that little old me that had always been told she wasn't good enough, who had failed at most things in life, could actually make something work; I could make a success of something.

And then, almost one year into my business, something happened. I found out that whilst I was trying to build this business up, yet another affair had been going on behind my back for months. When I found out, I was obviously crushed at first, as I suppose there was always that part of me that hoped things would change. Realistically it never would, but something was very different within myself this time. Before, I would have listened to the lies and the promises, but now my self-worth was starting to come back, and I knew with absolute certainty that I did not need this life that wasn't serving me, nor did I want it, because I deserved more and I owed myself more. I had a great business and financially I was doing well. I could support me and Lyla alone, I didn't need to put up with being treated like this, and I didn't need to stay somewhere that was not meant for me. My little girl was growing older and watching everything around her and it was more important to me for her to have good examples around her and a calm environment and to show her that women do not need to stay where we are not being treated like we deserve, that we can be independent, and I was going to give her the best life possible, no matter what, because that little girl that saved me deserved more too.

So I set myself free of the chains, I allowed myself to grow, to begin to heal, to find myself again. I allowed myself to be myself again without being controlled or criticised. I learned how to live life on my terms and to enjoy every minute of it. I loved taking my daughter away on trips and holidays, just us, and showing her the world. I felt so proud that I was able to do it on my own and it was the most freeing feeling I had ever experienced, being able to take control of my life. And then I started to receive messages from other single mums that had seen my travels with Lyla to say how scared they were to go away alone with their children but seeing me do it had inspired them to do it too, and my heart would just burst with love and pride – this alone made everything worth it.

My business also continued to grow, and I continued to grow with it.

I had so many friends and such amazing support around me now and my mind was in a completely different place – I had learned to look at positives of even the worst situations and so this to me was the beginning of the rest of my life; the one where I took the disasters life had thrown at me and began to see them differently. I began to view them as lessons. Yes, life is short and can end at any time – so enjoy it to the fullest while you're here; time spent worrying is time wasted and we worry about so much in life, all the while not realising life is passing us by. Life can and will happen to us all, times will get hard, and disasters and trauma will happen. We will feel like we have hit absolute rock bottom but rock bottom teaches you lessons that mountain tops never will – and once you've survived it once you know you can do it again. Healing from trauma for me doesn't mean forgetting it or going back to the old you, but learning to find new strength, joy and wisdom and moving forward with courage.

In any given moment, we can learn to rise and completely reinvent ourselves. It doesn't matter what's happened in the past or what we've done, we can learn new skills, new thought patterns and become the best versions of ourselves. Lots of us are told throughout our lives that we are not good enough, and we play this over and over in our heads until we believe it and we stay stuck where we are, but here's the thing: no one can really make you feel that way without your permission. You can't change how people behave towards you, but you can – and should – choose to walk away from it, it's essential for your growth.

Every one of us have always had what it takes to heal, to rise, to do better and grow inside of us all along – sometimes it takes something that presents you with no other option than to survive or thrive, like in my case my daughter – but the tools we need are always inside of us; the person we want to become is in there and there is a magic that happens when you begin to believe that you are enough. Alone or not, you can rise up.

All you can change is yourself, but sometimes that changes everything.

★★★

Maggie lives in Reading UK and is a single parent to one little girl, Lyla. She is a travel business coach and when she isn't busy mentoring her team you'll find her and Lyla off exploring the world.

You can find Maggie here:

https://www.facebook.com/maggie.byron
https://www.instagram.com/jetset_queen/
https://www.instagram.com/jetset_queen/maggie_byron

THE WAKE UP CALL
Sabrina Gendron

This chapter is for every server and bartender who has been stiffed a tip, left in the weeds of life and was made to feel you're worth less than 20%. It's time to become who you truly are and believe deep within your soul you deserve everything your heart desires.

"Whenever I call you, you're drunk or hungover! What's going on with you, girl?!"
— My best friend

You'd think that would have got me to check-in with myself and think about making some changes in my life, wouldn't you? But it didn't. I quickly phased out the reality-check my friend had just given me and clocked-in to my double weekend shift knowing that I was still going to have a lot more to drink by the end of it.

There's no way to sugarcoat this. I was drinking whenever I got the chance and didn't stop just because the bar closed. Knocking back generously-poured cocktails and slamming back shots was like self-medication to numb the pain. To everyone partying around me, it just looked like I knew how to have a good time. But this was my secret, of how I was hiding from the embarrassment, shame and disappointment I had of myself. My past failures had brought me to my knees. I'd put my hands in the air and given up. I stopped caring what was going to become of me. Which is how I ended up being in the hospitality industry for so long. I didn't plan on it, it sort of happened in a blur and my misguided soul put herself there until I got out of the drunken slum I was stuck in.

While I was there, I loved being in the hustle of the industry. Thriving in its fast pace and chaos of people from all walks of life coming and going. Keeping up with the rushes and serving as many people as possible in the time I was scheduled. I was hyper-confident in my customer service persona but was paralysed by fear of doing anything else other than hospitality. After ten years, it was all I had real experience in. So, I had created a buffet of self-doubt, crushing my self-esteem of who and what I could do otherwise to get out. Tiresome excuses and the soul-destroying lack of my self-worth were the high points of conversation for my pity-parties, catered with a display of cheap wine and comfort food. I had isolated myself from my friends, keeping myself to small groups of similar folks, who also liked a good time drinking, so my cover wasn't blown.

Wasting five years drowning myself in alcohol, cigarettes and hangover food, I was in the worst shape I'd ever been in my life. At the time, being inspired to refill my dreams for the future wasn't my vibe. It was easier to refill my drink and distract myself from facing what I had to do to fix it. My anxiety walking into every shift not knowing how much I was going to walk out with was putting serious money stress on my nerves, which caused me to drink. The more times I was stuck there with no customers, making no tips, boiled my frustration. All I wanted to do was walk out and quit. So I could have a drink. My thick skin was wearing thin with rude customers, who made me want to throw a drink in their face, but had to tolerate their bullshit with a Barbie smile. The final straw was having teammates that didn't want to be there even more than me. Who let their attitude show in their work ethic, leaving me to pick up the slack with customers, to cover their asses, to make sure we all still got the tip! I was at breaking point and a drunken rampage was soon to follow!

After every one of these explosive drunken episodes, I'd lost respect for myself. I didn't know when to stop and saw a side of me I never want you to meet. I wasn't sure how I was going to make it. I stopped believing I deserved to have the life I daydreamed about. I worked every hour I could possibly get and yet I was always about broke. Living day by day, scraping together what I could, just to get by, it felt like as soon as I earned it, it was out of my hands again. I just couldn't get ahead and after passing out on the bathroom floor, it was clear to me it was because I wasn't good enough to have more.

I had practiced an Oscar-winning performance of "I'm fine" just to get through the day. Because saying

"I don't know what I did to deserve this and would you mind if I just curled up in a ball right here, and cried my body to sleep and pretend it's all a nightmare" was going to create an awkward silence no one likes to be in the middle of.

There was no talent scout coming by to pick me out of the line up to save me. Staying in the industry, I'd lost focus of what I wanted for my future and got comfortable sticking to what I knew. My bubbly personality made it look like everything was 'hunky dory'. No one knew I had a problem, but me. And I knew many years from now I would regret giving up on having the self-worth and confidence to be the woman that changed her story to the epic one I'd longed it to be.

If you're not blinded by booze, there's a chance every day to do something about it. I was always only a swipe and a scroll from tapping into exciting opportunities and people ready to support me all over social media. And there were even people I'd met in my social butterfly days, who had used them to turn their lives around. I got that impulsive nudge that this was what I needed to do to turn the tables of my life. I wanted to be excited about life again and start totally loving me because of what I was doing every day. They knew how to get what I wanted and all I had to do was ask to learn from them how to go about getting it for myself. But I just didn't have the confidence to see myself doing what they were doing, so I went and made myself a drink to forget about it. That's when my confidence hit an all-time low!

You wouldn't have noticed any of this was happening to me, as every time I clocked-in, I was proving to the world that I could be doing something more than I was! Treating every customer I served like it was my own business, I carried with me a sense of pride and ownership in setting a high standard of serving when helping somebody. Even though I drank, I didn't let it affect my work and always showed up for other people. Yet I couldn't show up for myself. Why was this? I was serving other people better than I was serving myself. Why was I making me wait? When I wouldn't have dared expect any of my customers to wait for something they wanted, that I had to give them.

So I poured myself a drink and started brainstorming everything my years in hospitality had given me. When you do this, minus the alcoholic beverage by the way, you'll see that you've totally been underestimating what you're capable of. There are so many valuable qualities and unique talents you developed walking the walk of the industry. It was exciting to see that everything it put me through had been preparing me for this moment. For the first time in years, I felt valuable. My drive and ambition for life was coming back now I'd given myself credit for who I had become. What I had discovered was that a hospitality expert had the makings of a modern-day entrepreneur.

This was when I couldn't bear the heart and gut-wrenching feeling of remaining where I was any more! I wanted to live an incredible life and I was going to find out how to have the confidence and courage to get it!

It was time to focus on what will get me away from the toxic environment, clean up my act and prove that I can be more than what I was showing up as. It was time to take what I thought had been my disadvantage and make it a superpower.

At my next shift, I couldn't get the idea of becoming what my inner voice started calling a 'serverpreneur' out of my head. There was something else calling me now and it wasn't happy hour! I hadn't felt so empowered to make a positive change for myself in such a long time. My instincts were fired up and their sense of knowing was back! The conviction with which it was telling me to listen to these vibrant new thoughts, over the ones telling me to have a drink and not bother, made me trust that this was the right decision for me. It was time to say goodbye to the bullshit tearing me down. Quit beating myself up over every mistake I'd ever made and begin talking to myself with respect again. This was the wake up call to getting my confidence back and stand up for myself to see through the transformation I was ready to let myself have. It was time to put the bottle down!.

Drinking would bring out my paranoid thoughts and feelings that fueled my insecurities and anger. I'd trashed, smashed, hit, slammed, hospitalised myself, passed out on a stranger's couch, and spent the entire day in a dark room with my head in a toilet. Keeping this up was not the makings of the empowering serverpreneur I was prepping myself to be. Repeating my lowest moments over and over again wasn't going to grow my online empire successfully. It was clear if I kept doing what I was doing, I was going to keep getting the same results over and over again. I had to quit my drunken mess and it wasn't easy. I just kept telling myself, "If you want this enough, you'll do it." My sobriety has given me a clearer future, laser-like focus and lets me show up as the best version of myself for me and others to benefit from, and I can still show you a good time!

The worry hanging over me was the fear of someone exposing me or finding out about my dark past. Well, that was until I saw how much that overthinking was costing my future happiness. I needed to surround myself with inspiring like-minded people who believed in me, valued and understood how it was possible for someone like me to go and change their life for the better. The 'power takers' had no place in the future, I saw for myself. I couldn't let the remarks from others stand in my way of breaking free of the vicious cycle I'd caught myself in. To create the confident version of myself I saw escaping the soul-destroying hospitality industry, and launching an online business serving others on a larger scale. I needed an upgraded self-image that was so powerful that I couldn't doubt my abilities to do it! I chose to acknowledge the sharp, multi-talented solution finder I'd seen in action busting her ass off every hectic double weekend shift. She was going to be the one to make shit happen and confidently thrive in the new-age way of serving online!

I want you to get this, so you never let anyone stop you from going for what you truly want in life. Letting how other people make you feel shouldn't determine who you see yourself to be. That doesn't come from what anybody else thinks of you or the terrible parts of your past you need to let go of, but from the image you choose to have of yourself right now. Has anyone told you that you're allowed to have incredible beliefs in yourself? I know there's a long list of things that make you an outstanding awesome person. You reading this book already shows that you know there is something you have within you to unleash onto the world. Being open and excited to the possibilities for change tells you that there is something else you feel you were meant to do here. Next time you have an impulse to do something that will change your situation, choose an empowering thought about yourself that serves you best to do it confidently. You'll give your self-image a powerful sense of self-worth that no one can penetrate! And if anyone makes you feel any different or tells you that it's not possible... RUN! Read this part of the chapter until you feel like you can do it again. Because you can, you're going to make it, you've been through worse before. So go for it and don't stop until you get it!

This was 'the shift' I had been waiting for! And it was the one I was really going to make bank on. Now knowing if I wanted a dramatic lifestyle change, I was responsible for getting it. If I didn't do something about where my story was going, it was going to have a tragic end and not the epic one I felt I was destined to have.

My online business saved me. If I only had that bar job to go to, I wouldn't have anything to strive for that didn't make me reach for a drink. It's given me a fresh start, changed my unhealthy lifestyle and transformed me into the confident woman I am today. Being part of the online revolution gave me the mindset, attitude, exciting new skills, and most thankfully incredible supportive friends and mentors that have all given me a reason to survive. That's why I want to help those in the hospitality industry that are going through the same situation to know there is a way out. I know you didn't intend to be there this long. So, I'm gonna call you out and sense that you're not fine, and you're looking for an escape plan. Trust your gut! You are worth the amazing life you daydream of, rolling hundreds of silverware every day. Discover life after the industry, if it's become unhealthy for you mentally and physically. Serve yourself better, so you can serve more with a real impact on their lives and yours!

Until you do it, you'll always wonder: 'what if?!' I want this to have opened your eyes that you have what it takes to be an empowering online serverpreneur in the digital era of serving online. No more pity-parties, my friend! We are going to show up and make something of ourselves. Find the community that will help you, there's one in this book calling to you, so go check it out. Hang out with people that have what you want, are showing you how to get it and share the passion and excitement for what's possible with you. Get ready, get your shit together, down a protein shake and let's go!

You're worth more than 20%!

★★★

Sabrina's raw passion and gift for serving others started as a waitress in a cocktail bar in London,UK over a decade ago, putting hospitality in her blood.

When she's not serving customers or fellow Serverpreneurs, she focuses on serving herself with a holistic healthy lifestyle that gives her the confidence and empowerment to follow her calling.

She enjoys living life in the moment and loves spending time with ambitious go-getters, hungry for change.

Sabrina's committed to showing you how to believe in yourself and what can happen when you don't give up and go after what you truly want in life.

You can find Sabrina here:

http://bit.ly/JointheServerpreneursSociety
http://bit.ly/FindOutHowSabrinaCanServeYou
www.instagram.com/serverpreneurs_society

DIFFERENT IS GOOD
AND PAIN IS POWER

Chanelle Fry

This chapter is dedicated to my beautiful little family. My son Finlay who turned my world upside down and is my reason for everything. I want you to know that you are so special and can achieve absolutely anything you put your heart and soul into. To Terry, my husband, thank you for putting up with my craziness and creating a legacy business with me for our family. Love you both dearly.

I remember feeling like an outsider. It's hard to explain but for those of you that read this and have felt it you will know exactly what I mean… just an uneasy feeling of not fitting in and being a little bit 'different'.

My childhood was pretty crazy. My mum became a single parent when I was about ten and, rather than crumble from the crap she'd been dealt, she turned the whole experience into power for her and for us. My two sisters, mum and I became the best of friends and we learnt together how powerful a woman on the rise can be. I know it wasn't easy for my mum (being an empath), but we actually had the best time, we were like a girl gang!

At eleven, I went to a Catholic convent girl's school. I had a great group of friends that I adored, yet I was still bullied. There was one girl that made my life hell. I'm sure a lot of you reading this have had it worse, so I don't like to dwell on it, but the verbal abuse she gave me used to make me physically sick. I didn't show it, though, my friends and I would laugh it off and we'd say how "she just hates me", but it wasn't normal. We didn't know each other; she was just in my year and we had never really spoken. Still to this day I don't know what started her abuse, but now I realise wholeheartedly that behaviour was only her insecurities and really nothing to do with me at all! The problem is as kids we don't know that, and we do look internally and question *what the hell is wrong with me?!*

That was the narrative of my entire journey into adulthood really...

Why do I feel like I'm different? What's wrong with me?

Between this and things at home, I became pretty socially anxious. But nobody would have believed that for a minute! I took on a loud and outgoing personality and seemed extroverted. I was the absolute life and soul of the party. At sixteen I was like a girl on self-destruction mode. Out drinking at night clubs, staying out all night and getting up to all sorts of shenanigans. I'm sure lots of you reading this went through that stage too, but internally I was covering up my emotions with over-compensating and pretending everything was okay.

I left school to study fashion. My dream was to be a

fashion designer and, despite the lack of work I'd done to get there, I sailed into the college I wanted. But I didn't settle down, I just wanted to party and barely attended the lessons or even finished the two-year course.

My then boyfriend had no aspirations in life and together we wasted away the days.

A couple of years went by where I was suffering inside. I was functioning but not really living. Somehow, I'd managed to blag myself a place on a part-time degree at the London College of Fashion and a new job in a bank. Externally things were looking up, but my head was still a mess, I still felt alone and different and struggled to fit in at university. To be honest, I didn't really try… my lack of caring said it all, I had lost my spark.

Life continued like this until the boyfriend I was living with did something that changed my life. He cheated on me and it was the best thing he ever did.

Of course, I was hurt and at the time felt like I would never trust another man again, but very quickly I came to the conclusion it was time to change everything.

So, I picked myself up and got my shit together.

Over the next couple of years, I started making changes. Things weren't perfect but they were a hell of a lot better and, although I'd screwed up my degree by flunking out at the final hurdle, I had a good enough job and my health and my spark was coming back. That inner voice that had always spoken to me was getting louder, telling me I could achieve great things.

It's funny how the universe guides you! Not long

after this, one of my girlfriends took me for a night out and we bumped into some old friends of ours. One of them was Terry... now my husband and business partner!

Life was getting exciting! We fell madly in love and built a life together.

At twenty-six I fell pregnant and we were so happy. It felt like everything was falling into place for us... financially we were in a mess, but we were broke and happy.

The happiness made way for new emotions too and I began to feel ambitious again and take notice of the fire that was starting to burn bright inside of me. The positive changes were addictive to me, but I didn't know which direction to take. I always had a head for business and making money and had a 'side hustle'. I needed to! Even more so when I became a mum. It's one thing being broke when it's only you that might go hungry, but being responsible for another human being is a whole new ball game. That was the fuel to my fire.

I'd tried traditional businesses, hairdressing, events – I even set up a vintage fashion shop in London with my mum – and then I came across the network marketing business model.

I know there are always mixed feelings on this type of business and I'm not here to change your mind, but what I will say is I am forever grateful that I opened my mind to something different. It literally changed my life.

I began my career in the industry around six years ago when I actively sought out a new opportunity and there it was. It was selling a well-known aloe vera product and I loved it! One of my main reasons for joining (other than money) was to find new friends and people on my wavelength and it gave me that in abundance. Suddenly, I was surrounded by people just like me. Other mums that knew there was more to life than they had experienced up until now. I couldn't believe that there was a whole community of women that were so similar to me, and I loved being in groups with people that were on a journey to escape the 'norm'. Lots of them had similar stories to mine and had gone through their own life feeling like an outsider too.

For me, the beginning of my entire self-development journey to success started the day I made the decision to say yes. I'm not saying it happened overnight, in fact far from it. I always tell people I "failed" my way to success because I did. It took me many times in business getting it wrong to get it right. The first couple of years were more finding myself, which was a whole new world to me but one that was welcomed. I was so hungry for knowledge and I latched on to any tips and trainings that I could from people that I looked up to.

So here I was on this new journey that was bettering myself and my family, but the problem was the results weren't coming and so, to those around me, it seemed that I was "wasting my time". If you are on your own journey to building a successful business, I can pretty much guarantee you've heard this too and I want to tell you that it's okay, they don't understand. They don't have to right now and they will in time. You can't force people to see what you see! Network marketing is known for this attitude from others because it still can hold negative connotations (think eighties pyramid schemes!). It really just stems from a lack of understanding. Just be okay with it. I've had it all, lost friends, people telling me I'd joined a cult (that one still makes me laugh because if being in a cult means surrounding yourself with positive minds all on a journey to better themselves then that's a cult I'd happily join).

Thank God I didn't listen to the doubters around me and, to be honest, I can't blame them for their feelings. I joined three companies in my first four years and had zero success. It wasn't exactly matching what I was saying I was doing and achieving big things; but I truly believed beyond doubt that I would change my life. I remember one summer morning, I was standing in the kitchen making tea and Terry and I were disagreeing about the amount of time I spent on my phone and I looked him dead in the eye and said to him, "I'm going to change our lives through network marketing." Terry remembers it too. I didn't have all the answers, the strategies and definitely not the results, but I had grown an unwavering level of self-belief.

I finally felt like I belonged somewhere. This was the industry for me! It was exciting, inspiring and was helping me regain all the confidence and sparkle back that I had lost along the way.

I became like a human sponge, soaking in everything I could. I learnt by following the lead of those in my industry that had achieved great things. Don't get me wrong, there were bad habits along the way! Some of the strategies I was exposed to were quite honestly dreadful and that's the stuff that really doesn't help the industry's name; but I was savvy enough to cut through the crap and pull together the good stuff and it worked. I became really strong at marketing and I worked every day mastering that.

In June 2017, I came across an opportunity that I fell in love with. The product was travel and I could build a team. I jumped head in and made a decision that this was going to be my time. I applied all the stuff I'd learnt, and I became obsessed. In order to create huge success in your business you've got to give it your all. But here's the hook: if you are building a business you are truly passionate about, you will be. The early mornings, late nights and every moment you have in between you will want to be knee-deep in your business activities and the consistency and action will be there, if you really are aligned with what you are doing.

My obsession for building my business paid off. Now over two years in, my life is pretty unrecognisable. I built a six-figure income in year one and multiple six-figures in two years. Terry did a complete U-turn on the industry and is now my business partner! If you ask him what changed, he would say it was me! I stopped talking about what I was going to do and I just did it. Actions speak louder than words and my results couldn't be argued with. Together we were able to sack our bosses and start living our dream life. We became number one in Europe, won multiple awards, paid off all our debts, put our son in private school and have travelled the world together as travel coaches.

The best part is that now I get to make an impact. Once you start achieving your own goals and dreams you can start helping others and that's the best feeling in the world. Helping others should be on your list of priorities in your business. Whatever business you are in, be clear from the start on the impact you want to make and how your business mission can help other people. Any good business acts to serve others and that's something that will stand you apart from the rest.

It's not all been roses, even in these past two years. I know the struggle and frustration that can come with building a business. But honestly, I know for a fact that if I can do it you can too. Remember to follow that inner voice, your intuition won't lead you wrong, and be prepared for the work that a wildly successful business brings because it's not easy. In fact, it's one of the hardest things I've done, and I still face some of those old battles I did when I was younger. I've faced attacks from trolls and online bullies and the anxiety still rears its ugly head now and again, but I'm better equipped to deal with it and there's one thing I know to be true: broke and unhappy was just as hard (if not harder). I know which hard I choose every damn day. How about you?

Life is there for the taking. There are no dress rehearsals so be real and ask yourself: 'Am I serious or am I playing?' Get serious about your goals and create a clear and beautiful vision for your life. What will you be doing in five years' time? Where will you live? What will you have done? Who will be around you? How many people will you have helped along the way? These visions need to be so clear it's like you could touch them. Then you need to get to work. It's yours for the taking, there is no time for excuses. We all have a story but turn yours into your power and go and fight for your vision.

That pain you feel now, the frustration and anger and feelings of not understanding is all okay. There will always be people around you that don't understand you and vice versa. They don't need to understand you and you don't need to understand them! You just need to focus on what's important to you. Those that have negative opinions and bully or hate on you have their own issues. *It's not you. It's them.*

You are going to have a great life… it might be hard to see now but you are. You have the power to change your life and you will. That inner voice that you have is your best friend. Listen to it more as it's guiding you on the right path. Oh, and enjoy the journey… there is so much in store for you.

★★★

Chanelle's love for helping female business owners build a passion-led business has meant she has been able to have an impact on and empower thousands of femalepreneurs across the globe. When she isn't coaching women online she spends her time travelling the world with her family, speaking at international events and developing a winning mindset. Chanelle's committed to helping people create a freedom lifestyle and focuses her work on helping people create a brand that creates massive visibility and impact on social media; she believes that everybody has the opportunity and ability to create their dream business and that it's never too late nor never too early to go for what you want in life.

You can find Chanelle here:

www.ChanelleFry.com
Facebook.com/ChanelleFryCoaching
Instagram.com/ChanelleFryCoaching

Be the Reason They Won't Quit

Di Carter

This chapter is dedicated to women who are fighting to be heard in a noisy world of femalepreneurs, who are a positive influence wherever God takes them.

Part 1: "Bless the world with your story, share the light God gave you"

I came from a small poor village in Brazil, going to England, cleaning a lot of toilets along the way and landing in the United States with $100 in my pocket. You get the picture, right?

My life wasn't easy, and I am sure yours hasn't been either. We all face many struggles and fears through this journey we call life. I had to fight against the odds of success.

You might see yourself throughout my story and the connection you will feel is real. Take a deep breath and enjoy it. This exercise will clear your mind and make you smile.

Here are a few questions you might have as you start this chapter. Who is the girl who cleaned toilets? What can I learn from her story? Why would our journey be similar?

Keep reading so you can be blessed today. Open your heart and enter the world of your imagination. Let me take you back to where it all began!

My name is Di Carter; I am a serial entrepreneur and a network marketing professional. Today, I will share a piece of my heart with you.

I was born in Brazil, raised by an eighteen-year-old single mom and babysitter who made me feel like a princess every day, even though we didn't have any money. Life from the get-go was not the perfect family picture and I grew up without my biological father.

I came from a very poor family where having shoes and new clothes were a luxury. We all learned quickly how to make our own toys with plastic bottles and had to be satisfied with what we had to eat.

My mom stopped going to school in the fourth grade so she could help her family. I am not ashamed of my mom's past. In fact, I am very proud of her for doing all she could to break the chain of poverty with no education.

Age ten: my life changed dramatically. Why? My mom found the perfect man. "A well-respected gentleman", a senator. My life began to change. I went to the best school from that point of my life and no one knew my story. I remember vividly being around the most educated, well-dressed kids with well-known names when my last name meant "poverty, broken family, no future".

Early on, I knew I wanted to have an impact on many lives. I just didn't know how.

Ten – fifteen years old: I donated all of my expensive toys and fancy clothes to the kids in the village.

I remember saving my lunch money so I could take all the kids in the village to eat ice cream. It felt so good to be able to give to the ones that had nothing. I can't put into words their appreciation for being able to enjoy the things we take for granted.

Imagine getting your favourite toy at Christmas; that was how they felt.

Those moments had an impact on my life and I felt the urge to create something. I believe those were the early stages of my entrepreneurial mind.

I used to wonder how I could do more for the less fortunate. What would I do if I had the opportunity to create something bigger than myself?

The word impact never left my soul to do more for others

At fifteen, I had my first encounter with Jesus. From that point on, everything changed for anyone who would be around me.

At sixteen, I landed in the USA as an exchange student. I only knew how to say, "How are you?" "I am hungry," and "Where is the bathroom?"

Wow... how did I get here? I remember being inside of an airplane for nine hours, saying, "Commit to the

Lord whatever you do, and your plans will succeed." Proverbs 16:3.

I learned how to speak English, I had an impact on many lives and I felt so happy. I was fascinated with American culture.

It was time to go back to Brazil and, this time, my stepdad was sick with diabetes and no longer had money to help with my education.

At eighteen, I had an opportunity to go to England to work. The goal was to clean toilets for six months at Home Depot and pay for my flight attendant school.

WHAT A DREAM!!! If all worked out, I'd be able to travel the world.

At nineteen, I landed in the USA with $100 in my pocket. What I knew for sure: God had a plan for me all along. I got married, divorced and lost all my friends from high school. When all the twenty-one-year-old kids were celebrating having their first drink, I was feeling alone and had no hope for the future.

Fast forward to seven years later and I am a flight attendant. Who would have thought a little girl from a poor village would be travelling the world, getting a degree, and marrying a pilot?

Pinch me! He is a God of second chances!

PART 2: How BIG IS YOUR FAITH?

At thirty I became a mom of two beautiful blonde-haired and blue-eyed twin girls and I am a true Latina. Picture this: I get asked at least once a month if I am my girls' babysitter, I have dark brown hair, dark skin and dark eyes.

Once I became a mom, my life as a surgical technologist didn't make any sense any more. I needed to find a way to stay home and find that balance that I always wanted.

At this point in my life, I had my second encounter with Jesus.

I called this the point of our lives where we start seeing the blessings. Think back on your life to where everything started to click and started to make sense. I finally understood the meaning of impact, the burning desire to do and be more. I knew there was something out there for me. "Where God guides, he provides." Isaiah 58:11

At thirty-two: I was working full-time as a surgical technologist in the OR on my feet, fatigued, overweight and unhappy with my health. I couldn't take one more day waking up at 5am and feeling like a number at work. What I really didn't like was not being able to kiss the boo-boos 24/7. I was seeing my family through my cell phone pictures more than in real life.

Just by telling you my story, it hurts to know that I wasted so many of those precious moments. If only I made the decision sooner to follow God's gifts, I wouldn't be in tears when I tell you my story.

I found a way to work my own hours and build a network marketing business. I knew it wouldn't be fast, but I have twins and with that I learned how to be patient.

I couldn't quit my job right away, so I kept working until the time was right. I was a workaholic, so God had to intervene. I got fired and I was grateful that I was building my plan B, C and D.

"I will walk by faith even when I cannot see." 2 Corinthians 5:7

PART 3: THE SHOCKING TRUTH ABOUT SOCIAL MEDIA AND ENTREPRENEURSHIP

We called it "the new gig social economy", where we don't need to leave the house to make connections to the outside world.

Do you currently use any of those apps? Facebook, Instagram, Uber, Amazon, YouTube, Airbnb?

What does it mean to be a social entrepreneur?

It means to be able to influence your network by using social media, to create a greater impact while having fun making an income. You find the needs of society and you are providing the solution to their problems.

So, how did I have an impact on thousands of people spiritually, financially and mentally? I hope today you can understand the power of social media and how much you can have an impact on the world with your ideas and dig into your creative side. Let's start!

Spiritually – How many people are heartbroken?

We know that hurt people hurt more people, but broken crayons still colour. In 2013, I went to a women's conference where the speaker was Lisa Harper, who is a well-known Christian motivational speaker. I left that conference with a vision from God. "For I know the plans I have for you." Jeremiah 29:11.

I spent a few weeks brainstorming how I would have an impact on my community in a positive way. As I was listening to Christian radio, the idea came to my mind. I had an 'aha!' moment, a whisper in my ear: "You found your calling." It was clear. I heard: "Child, you are going to organise a Christian concert for hundreds of heartbroken people to worship my name."

Being a new mom of twin girls, I couldn't leave my house, but I knew with social media I could reach out to thousands of people in my community.

I started by creating a name for the event, a logo and a website. I researched online how to promote, find sponsors, sign contracts and finally a place to hold the event. It took a lot of faith to bring my vision alive and it took social media to plant the mustard seed.

I created a business page where I built an audience of fanatical Christian fans and non-believers.

Christ Fest PC was born in 2013. I started to attract more people using my profile page by posting weekly and sharing my journey along the way.

God opened the doors and brought a beautiful young

lady named Rachel Jervis, who was the brains behind the scenes.

After six months of planning, working hard and putting endless hours on this vision, I found myself lying on the floor of my bedroom praying to God: "Lord please help me, I built it, now it's your turn to show up." All I could hear was, "You did well, my child."

Here are the results: our first concert had 500 people; our second concert had 900 people.

Today over seventy people from various churches around my small town have volunteered at Christ Fest. We had our fourth Christian concert last summer, and we have had an impact on thousands of lives and many broken people have been saved. "Your vision matters, everything matters." Di Carter.

Can I get an Amen?

I understood the power of Social media and a Christian social entrepreneur was born.

Financially – How can I have an impact on more lives with all this knowledge I learned from Christ Fest?

In 2016, I learned how to manage a team of volunteers, how to motivate them and what it takes to grow a non-profit organisation.

I have always wanted to open a business. Once again, I turned to social media, where I found a few business friends and started asking questions. I had 30k in a 401k from a previous employer that I could transfer to my husband's 401k or invest in my own start-up business.

After seeing the results of my social entrepreneur adventure, I realised that I could do it again!

I went to Brazil, South America, did my research and found a niche market that needed a distribution centre to supply the small businesses with their cleaning products, equipment and office supplies.

Let me explain: we don't have Walmarts or Sam Club in every small town in Brazil. I found the solution for a problem!

I started the whole process again: name of the company, logo, business plan, hiring people, financial planning and inventory. I had to travel to Brazil a few times. We built a company from the ground up to a seven-figure business. Pinch me! It was not an overnight success, this moment over here calls, "My vision matters, and God is my anchor."

The decisions were made through my smartphone using WhatsApp, Facebook and Skype.

I understood the power of social media and the CEO of Qualimax do Brazil was born.

Mentally – How could I simplify social media for women like me?

I wasn't done with social marketing. This was my third business and I chose network marketing.

Social media success formula:

1. Tell stories (create the trust and likeability factor).
2. Share the products/opportunity (curiosity post).
3. Ask the question and let them decide.

My biggest answer when people ask: 'what do you do'? "I use social media to create a second income." Di Carter.

The truth is, it takes guts to go after your dreams when others are watching you struggling and hoping that you fail. It takes perseverance and coaching from people like Eric Worre, Ray Higdon and Femalepreneurs Academy. When the student shows up, so does the teacher.

Are you coachable? Can you see your future? What do you care more about, your bank account being ZERO or what others think of you? As a social entrepreneur, you will get a lot of no's.

You will be developing your communication skills, mindset and lastly influence. That is when you will have an impact on dozens, hundreds, thousands or even millions.

Everyone with any level of experience can do it.

Reality check question: are you willing to put yourself out there and tell your story to attract your perfect people?

On that note, in case you say, 'I don't know anyone!' Think again, there are two billion people on Facebook alone praying that you become an example for them.

Did you know I live in a small town with 1400 people in total?

There is no stop light. There is no convenience store. There is no gas station. There is no elementary school, and guess what? There is no food delivery.

Explain to me, why can't you build an online business?

I keep reminding myself that I came from poverty. Nothing will stop me! What is your why? Dig deep, girl!

Don't get me wrong, I know what God has in store for his children. When will you stop the self-doubt and start going through the failures? The only way to success is falling on your knees.

When will you realise that many people go online because they are spiritually, financially and mentally broken? How can you be the answer to their prayers?

The shocking truth about social media is to show up knowing that Facebook is your personal billboard, YouTube is your TV show and Instagram is the behind-the-scenes; use the stories.

What I know for sure is social entrepreneurship has been on the rise in the past five years and it's not going anywhere. What you create as a social entrepreneur is up to you.

Once I realised that my followers needed my services to help them create content, I opened a Facebook group/page and my website dicarter.com was born.

Following your passion will lead you where God wants you. Do you hear me, girl?

I understood the power of social media and the founder of social entrepreneur leaders was born.

"Whatever you do, do it with all your heart." Colossians 3:23.

In closing, I would like to invite you to live your

dreams. Do you accept the invitation? Can you feel in your gut that this is your time?

Today, I am a 24/7 stay at home mom, wife and businesswoman. I help many start-up businesses with creating content. Furthermore, I enjoy volunteering in my community and changing the lives of the less fortunate by going back to my country, Brazil, as a missionary to my people. That little girl found her calling.

What I know for sure is: God doesn't stop pursuing you; I give you permission to soar like an eagle.

★★★

Di Carter is a social and serial entrepreneur. She is described as an inspirational network marketing professional and is very passionate about her faith.

She believes you were made for more and that you can achieve anything you set your mind to. Your true calling in life is there for the taking if you truly want it!

When Di isn't running her successful businesses, you can find her spending time with her loving husband, her two beautiful twin girls and helping many of the less fortunate!

You can find Di here:

www.dicarter.com

www.Facebook.com/socialentrepreneurleaders

https://linktr.ee/dicarter.com_

Finding the Light Through the Dark

Emma Hammond

This is dedicated to anyone who has ever felt like they don't belong, and they aren't good enough; the misfits, the abused, the dreamers. May you always find the strength to take those risks and know there is always light again out there.

As I sat there in a pool of my own tears, clutching boxes of tablets, I was sure of two things. One, that I had nothing left of me to give at that moment; I had no energy, no joy, no light, nothing. I was exhausted beyond measure. And two, that I just wanted it to end. Did I want to die? I don't think so. I needed help. I just wanted everything to stop, the thoughts running through my mind, the pain, the despair, the loneliness, the emptiness.

When I was a child, I remember growing up and feeling like I was an alien on this planet. It was like I was living my life in a bubble. On the edge of everyone else, not quite able to touch them. They had this special secret, this language that I didn't understand. No one would tell me. Did I have to work out a secret code to be part of the gang and have friends?

Maybe if I was prettier, or smarter, they would like me? Maybe I just needed to dress more like them or talk more like them. Always feeling like I wasn't enough. The outsider.

So, I didn't talk, I shrank away into my own head. Left with my books and my fantasies. A magical world I created just for me. The only problem with that was that nothing was real and nothing real lived up to my fantasy life. I become more and more dissociated from reality.

As a teenager, alcohol and drugs were my friend. They numbed all the negative emotions of not feeling good enough, gave me confidence, helped me to reinvent myself. I was the life and soul of the party, everyone's friend. At the weekend, at the parties. They loved me, finally.

No one really knew me, though, not the real me. I was always trying so hard to be what everyone else wanted me to be. Trying desperately to fit in. Damn, I didn't even know myself. What was I passionate about? What were my values? What was even going on in my own head? What did I really want from life?

So, I drank all weekend, suffering terrible blackouts. I started waking up in places I didn't even recognise, with people I didn't even know, dealing with the beer fear. What the fuck did I get up to last night? Oh God, I hope I didn't embarrass myself too badly. Dealing with feelings of shame. Then came the come down all of Sunday and most of Monday.

It was back to work as a little worker bee, buzzing

away, doing what I was told, bored out of my mind. Society tells us that we should have a good job, though, right? Work nine to five, Monday to Friday, every week like clockwork. I lived for the weekend, counting the hours down until I could get out every day. So I could do what? Go home and watch Coronation Street and whatever other mind-numbing programmes were on the box that night that would distract me from my reality.

It's FRIDAY! Party time again! Just a hamster on a wheel.

Depression is something we are all familiar with, whether we have been touched by it ourselves, or know someone that has, but very often we don't even notice it staring us straight in the face. It is feeling tired and not knowing why, negative thoughts running through your mind, not wanting to speak to people, wanting to hide but at the same time desperate to connect with someone, anyone, just one person that understands you. It is lying all day in bed because you have a headache or you have a cold or some other imaginary illness you have convinced yourself that you have just so you don't have to get out of bed.

It is wishing for the light but being so scared of it you don't open your curtains for days. It is total darkness, total sadness, total loneliness. But whilst you are in it, you can't see it. You have no idea how to claw your way out of the darkness.

So when I sat there that day, at the age of twenty-nine, in my bed alone, curtains drawn, tears rolling and clutching those pills, it didn't occur to me that I was suffering from depression, that maybe talking about it could help me, that tomorrow would be another day and that the light would at some point come back into my life. I just saw darkness all around me. I was numb. I wanted it all to stop. I wanted to get off this ride called life.

After that trip to the hospital, the stomach pumping and a lot of time to myself to think, I realised that I never wanted to die, not really. What I wanted was a purpose, I wanted passion in my life, I wanted love, connection and happiness.

But I had built these walls up all around me that were so high no one could get in, not even a sledgehammer could bring them down. Not only did I block everyone else out, though, I was also blocking myself. I didn't have any love or compassion for myself, so every time someone who could be good for me got too close, I hurt them or sabotaged our friendship or relationship in some way or another.

It took some time, but slowly I started to see what I needed to do. The toxic relationship I was in ended and I took it as an opportunity for a fresh start. A new life, putting myself and what I wanted first.

I packed up and sold everything I owned with the exception of one suitcase of personal belongings and clothes. All the furniture in my two-bedroom house, gone, car, gone, job, gone, house, gone. I have never in my life felt so free. I had nothing, no stress, no debts, no material possessions, but I felt amazing.

I left everything behind and moved over from

Manchester to Jersey with my one suitcase and a clear mind. I already had some family living over there, though, so I wouldn't be completely on my own. I was going to move in with my dad, his wife and my stepsister.

It was a completely impulsive decision, but I was determined to make that move. It felt right, I was listening to my intuition and taking action quickly before the negative chatter started again. You know the negative chatter, the voices that tell you it's a bad idea, it's too risky, that there are lots of things that could go wrong. This time, though, it didn't stand a chance. Within weeks of making my decision to leave, I had sold everything I owned and was on a plane to start my new life.

I got a job and started making friends. It was different this time, though. I was actually making genuine connections. My walls had come down slightly and I started to let people in again.

I started a new relationship and very quickly found out I was pregnant. Not an ideal situation, but I don't regret any of it, even when I became a single parent when my baby boy was only five months old.

I don't think anyone ever sets out to be a single parent, and the challenges of single parenthood, well, I could write a whole book about that in itself. So I will just stick with saying that it has been incredibly challenging but also one of the most rewarding experiences I have ever had. I have had days when I want to scream and tear my hair out, but then he smiles at me or comes out with a smart remark that makes me laugh or he gives me a big hug and says, "I love you, Mum, you're the best," and I feel so proud of the incredible little man I am raising.

Living in Jersey had its challenges in itself: no benefits or support for me as a single parent as you have to live in Jersey for five years before you can claim anything. Rent is expensive, food is expensive, well pretty much everything is expensive compared to living in England, and I had to find a way to earn a living and look after and support my child at the same time.

So, I worked two part-time jobs and ran an online network marketing business in my free time; not that I had much time, but every second that I could. Thankfully I was blessed with a baby that slept, so when he was in bed at 7pm, I would get out my laptop and market myself and my products on social media to make some extra money to cover costs for food and bills.

I was working so hard, though, something had to give. I was on autopilot, powering through, looking after my baby, looking after my business and my clients, but not looking after myself. I didn't really understand what burnout was until it stopped me in my tracks.

My mind was on overdrive, battling with anxiety. I had no social life to speak of, just the baby and work. I didn't even realise that I had swapped one addiction for another. No more drinking and doing drugs, but an obsession with working. In the process of trying to create myself a life of freedom and give my son everything he deserved, I had completely lost myself again. I had no time for me, no time for my baby, I was running on empty.

Then it hit me, my body started to give up. It was crying out for rest. Infections, viruses, my body a swirling mass of pain. Every single muscle in my body ached to stop, to slow down. Then my vision went and the right-hand side of my body just seemed to shut down. It went completely numb and the right-hand side of my face dropped.

I was so scared. Nothing like this had ever happened to me before. I went to my doctor and straight away I was taken to hospital, concerned it might be something to do with my brain. Straight in for tests and brain scans and a week in hospital away from my baby.

Bell's palsy, they said it was. They don't know what actually causes it, but it's likely stress. My body just had enough and couldn't cope any more. I didn't know how to slow down and rest, so I was forced to stop. I certainly couldn't work for a while like that. I lost my smile, my trademark, which in turn knocked my confidence.

A true wake up call.

I started an online business so I could create more freedom in my life, work less and spend more time with my little boy and doing what I love, but it hadn't worked out that way.

What I learnt when growing up was that you had to work hard for your money; the more you worked the more money you made. But is that actually true? Surely there was an easier way, I just had to find it.

I took several months off to build myself back up again, get fit and healthy, get out of the depression I found myself in once more and start achieving all of the things I had promised to myself and my little boy.

I decided to launch my own business, using the skills I had picked up marketing myself through social media to teach others how to start building a freedom business. But this time I would do things differently.

I looked for ways to simplify and automate the processes in my business. I hired a business coach to help fill the gaps I was missing in my knowledge and I became obsessed with automation; chatbots, sales funnels, email marketing and any trick to save me time.

With the extra time I gained I could serve more clients and spend more time marketing and growing my personal brand.

In just two months, I had made my first 5K in my business and took one of the biggest risks so far.

I left my job, no idea how I would make a consistent income. It was all on me now. But I was free, I was happy, and I was so incredibly proud of myself.

Now I am a speaker, author and own a global digital marketing agency.

Looking back at my experiences is interesting. Remembering how low I felt at some points and that life wasn't worth living.

But my struggles got me to where I am today and for that I am incredibly thankful. Through struggle comes understanding. No matter what happens to you, you do have the strength to go on; humans are very resilient.

Don't try to push your pain away, it is part of you and it's there for a reason. It is there to teach you something and help you grow. Allow yourself to feel your emotions, to let them out and to share them with the people around you.

One of the biggest lessons I have learnt is that we aren't responsible for other people and their actions, we can only control our reaction to any situation. Change your perception and it changes everything.

I put too much thought into what others would think about me, I tried to fit in and trying so hard just pushed me further away from everyone else. You are unique, you are like no other person on the planet, don't try to hide yourself by being a boring version of everyone else.

You need to focus on you; what do you really love to spend your time doing? What type of people do you want to surround yourself with? Decide on the energy you want in your life and create it. Someone doesn't treat you with respect, you don't have to put up with it. You can say no, you do have a choice.

Remember that, no matter how dark things seem right now, there is always a light at the end of the tunnel. There are always people that will understand what you are going through, you just have to find the right people. Your people.

You really don't need to work so hard. If something is a struggle, listen. What is it trying to teach you? If something isn't working, change your strategy. Don't keep trying to do the same thing if it isn't bringing you the results you want or the life you want.

Another thing I discovered was that I have been making

everything far more complicated than it has to be most of my life.

Learn to love yourself, discover what makes you happy, spend more time doing the things that you love and spend more time with people that make you feel alive.

If you want something just go for it, don't live in fear of something not working out, you will always regret it if you don't take the risk.

★★★

Emma Hammond, AKA The Queen of Automation is a single mother living in Jersey, The Channel Islands.

She is a business consultant and runs her own digital marketing agency focusing on helping coaches and consultants create six-figure businesses working less than twenty hours a week.

When she isn't busy being a mother or business builder she loves to connect with nature, travel and enjoys a large glass of red wine and a home-cooked vegan meal.

You can find Emma here:

www.emmahammond.co.uk
https://www.facebook.com/elhammond1
https://www.facebook.com/groups/
CreatingFreedomForEmpoweredBusinessOwners

THE COMEBACK QUEEN
Tara Golino

*I dedicate this to my beautiful children, Destinee and Christian,
who are the reason I continue to push through all of life's lows
and never give up! They keep me grounded and remind me of
what is important and what is not. I never want them to look
back on their childhood and say, "Mommy did the best she
could." No. I want them to say, "Mommy couldn't have done
any better!"*

"What the F★ just happened?" I asked myself that exact question on an early morning in January. Within seconds of opening my eyes the flood gates of tears had opened and I found myself in hysterics. The first day of a New Year is generally a holiday when people are excited for new beginnings and setting goals for the upcoming months. Not me. Instead here I was, confused how I got to this place in my life. I was trying my hardest to silence my emotions in the hope to not wake up my kids. Christian, my five-year-old son, was sleeping next to me and Destinee, my twelve-year-old daughter, was sleeping in her room. I was super overwhelmed and felt trapped in our tiny 800 SqFt apartment. The last thing

I needed was either one of them waking up and seeing what a wreck I was.

Four months prior to this awful morning, the kids and I were living our BEST LIFE. We went from zero vacations to travelling every three months, from $300 a month in food stamps to dining at five-star restaurants a few nights a week. From hand-me-down clothes to shopping every chance we got! And let's not forget there weren't sounds of gunshots at night any longer since we had finally moved out of the projects and into the suburbs.

Growing up, I remember from a very young age, my mom was single, depressed, and had severe substance abuse. We received government assistance in literally ALL of the ways, no car, and we were constantly moving from one section eight apartment to the next. The worst one was the two-bedroom apartment in a crusty yellow house, located on a garbage lot, 20ft from the train tracks. It was very difficult for me to live under these conditions, which made me grow up way faster than most children my age. We lived in a very wealthy small town where everybody knew everybody and the majority of people, including my family and friends, were middle class or higher. Every school day I would walk onto the bus inundated with anxiety. I knew I would soon be getting off my stop and walking up the hill in the opposite direction until the bus was no longer in sight. My biggest fear was people knowing I lived there. Not only that, but I never knew what I was coming home to. My mom would either be in a delusional rage or passed out with her head between her knees with a lit cigarette in hand. Given the number of burn holes in the rug surrounding the spot she never moved from, it's unfortunate that the crusty yellow house didn't burst into flames.

When I was twelve years old, I attended a doctor's appointment with her. She was given the diagnosis of cirrhosis of the liver. The doctor explained the potentially fatal outcome if she did not stop immediately. Unfortunately, four years later, my mother entered into eternal rest. After years of self-reflection, I have realised that this tragedy and everything that led up to it was the beginning of my bad habit of "people pleasing" in an effort to feel accepted, wanted and loved. I had subscribed to an entire belief system of unworthiness, zero self-love, etc. and because of that I would put everyone else's feelings and situations before my own daily – and then would beat myself up for it too!

I'd always put other's feelings and situations before my own. Up until I was thirty-five, I would beat myself up on a daily basis for never having the courage to say no in fear of not being accepted. My mom's drinking caused me to feel unworthy of sticking around for, knowing that if she were to pass, I would be left alone in the world to fend for myself. My "dad" pretty much denied my existence until the age of twelve when he was forced by the State of Connecticut to take a paternity test; the test came back that he was 99.9% my dad, and he still chose not to have a relationship with me and still doesn't. (Insert hard eye roll.) Only now does it not affect me one bit.

After the passing of my mom, I was adopted by my aunt and uncle, but still felt extremely alone. I was in the most crucial years of my adolescence, but due to little to no guidance, lashing out and grieving my mom, my life lessons were learned the hard way. At twenty-one, I found out I was pregnant with Destinee. I had no business bringing a child into this world, but by the grace of God it was one of my greatest blessings to date. Being a mother taught me responsibility, unconditional love and motivated me like never before. Unfortunately, five weeks before I gave birth, her father was sentenced to four and a half years in jail and I was entering into the single mother life as a brand new mama. A little after Destinee's first birthday, we moved into low income public housing and that alone was a huge culture shock for me. I worked two jobs to put myself through college, interned at the State's Capitol for the General Assembly, a few different halfway houses, and for the Parole Department in Bridgeport. Five months prior to graduation, I found out I was pregnant again. I was thrilled to welcome the new baby and make Desi a big sister! One of my proudest moments was having Destinee by my side and Christian in my belly when I graduated with my bachelor's degree in Criminal Justice with a minor in Human Behaviour. The only problem was, three months before graduation, the state of Connecticut started laying off state workers. This meant that after four and a half years of time, studying, travel and $46,000 in student loans, the chance of being a parole officer was even further away. I didn't allow this to defeat me and continued working two jobs to make sure I gave my children the best life I possibly could.

About a year and a half after graduating, I had a breakdown. This is not what I had envisioned life to look like after graduation. I was so fed up with life and all of its constant detours that I lashed out and prayed. "God, I have done everything right, but somehow I keep falling short! It's my turn to excel in life! I am asking for an opportunity that will give me the chance to work hard BUT an opportunity that will pay off in a huge way. A life of time and financial freedom!

A few weeks later, I received a friend request on IG from a girl I didn't know. After a few weeks of watching her, I noticed that she was talking about a six-figure income she was earning from social media without a college degree! Clearly I was doing something wrong because I went to college, worked two jobs, and was nowhere close to six figures. I reached out to her for more information, and I joined the world of multi-level marketing knowing this was God's answer to my prayer.

When I started the business, I wasn't social media savvy at all, but I DECIDED that I would become a student of the industry. I didn't make any excuses, and began building my business. I hit the ground running and never looked back. After four months, I created a multiple four-figure income, quit my job, got off government assistance, and moved up out of the projects and into a new apartment in the suburbs. About a year later, during the holiday season, my income significantly dropped due to the ebbs and flows of MLM. I went from earning multiple four-figures per month down to $500 per month pretty much overnight. Just a few months later, in January, I found myself crying and hiding in the Department of Social Services because I didn't want anybody to see me in there applying for food stamps.

I felt like the world's biggest failure! But as I walked out of the building, I received a phone call from a girl that I had become friends with in the company. She presented me with an opportunity to join an exclusive upcoming beauty brand. I was both scared and reluctant to leave because it was all so sudden and I did have a team of 200 people I'd be leaving behind – something kept nudging me to take the risk on something new. There was only one problem. I didn't have enough funds to join! Christmas had just passed, my credit cards were maxed and my bank account was negative. Instead of going down the rabbit hole, I decided to just figure it out. I sold my household items for eighteen days until I came up with $333. I enrolled, and once again hit the ground running. Within five months, I created a five-figure monthly income. In nine months, I paid off the 46K in student loans, on my one-year anniversary I reached the top of the company and then went on to becoming the #19 income earner throughout all three countries. I achieved every incentive, ranging from the company car, trips, cash bonuses to recognition from the company.

I began one of the fastest growing teams and still to this date they are crushing!

The bliss I found in helping women reach their highest potential ignited my passion to help more women on a larger scale by helping them turn THEIR passions into profit. It was at that point that I began working on developing my own coaching business. The "plan" was to launch it that summer. For the first time in my life, I felt unstoppable and had reached a level of confidence that I had never experienced before; feelings of being accepted, loved, appreciated, valued and part of a mission much larger than myself. This would have been the perfect time to launch my personal brand since I was on cloud nine living my best MF life. Life was perfect, magical and beyond amazing, until it wasn't…

Sometime later, I was approached and presented with the opportunity to be part of a pre-launch. I had ZERO intentions of leaving where I was but after hearing more information I had agreed to meet with the CEO. After several meetings and everything sounding super intriguing, I decided to look into it. However, there was one big problem. I'd have to leave behind an incredible business I had built with people I deeply and genuinely love.

I didn't want to keep moving on to different businesses, but we don't make the ultimate plan, so we must follow the nudges! The day this person decided to leave for this new position, all hell broke loose and then I also resigned. Looking back, I can honestly say I allowed my ego and pride to interfere with making a concise decision but I believe everything happens for a reason and you have to follow your heart. Within a matter of twenty-four hours, I found myself in the centre of a smear campaign, unfollowed, blocked and all sorts of devastating actions against me. I know when people move on from network marketing ventures to the next, it can be rough, but I have always lived by integrity and I would never be malicious or intentionally hurt anyone. My heart was broken. I never anticipated any of this happening, especially from people whom I still love deeply.

At this point, there were many red flags that should have stopped me from pursuing the new venture. Despite the ongoing drama and the hurt that I endured from being outcasted by people I built valuable relationships with, I persevered. I did the first and most important step; I continued to show up because I HAD to. For myself and for my children! It was so challenging, but I worked hard and never gave up! In fifty-one days, I was the second person to reach the top of the company, earned close to six figures in bonuses and was the #2 income earner. While that sounds amazing on paper, I still had an unsettled knot in my stomach about my decision to join. The enticement that sparked my interest did not pan out. I learned a lot about people during this process and realised it was not what was presented. I began to go inward and became an outcast because I knew in my heart that I wasn't "home". I felt scared, stuck, alone and pulled every which way. I had major PTSD from all that I endured and it held me back from leaving. After ninety days of being there, some things had transpired and I went without pay for a few months. Talk about major feelings of regret, shame, fear for possible effects on my children, embarrassment and extreme self-doubt... hence why I woke up – at the start of my chapter – asking myself, how TF did I get here?! I did revisit the idea of launching my coaching business but I couldn't even fathom mustering up the courage to start it, especially since my confidence was little to non-existent.

Six months after the dreary self-loathing morning, I did my best to power through the best way I knew how until, one night, the feelings of being scared and stuck in a company I didn't want to be in, unworthiness, failure and guilt, flooded my body once again, but this time it hit way different and I broke down. In the midst, I heard a whisper that said, "Whatever happened to the girl in the bathtub filled with money back in January?"

It was the weirdest thing ever, considering I had unfollowed this woman on Instagram and never thought about her ever again until I heard a whisper. I have no doubt this was a Divine intervention. I am sure you are wondering why I unfollowed her in the first place and then thought about her again, right? Well, here's the deets. Shortly after we connected, she posted a picture of herself in a bathtub filled with $100 bills with a glass of champagne in hand. I can honestly say that it triggered TF out of me! All of my self-limiting beliefs around me and my paradigms around money came to light. Needless to say, thank God I had DM'd her back in January thanking her for the follow – otherwise I wouldn't have been able to find her because I couldn't remember her name to save my life. For the next three or four hours, I consumed every single piece of content she had available from her IG highlights, IGTVs, YouTube channel, business page and podcast! It was in those wee hours of the morning listening to her speak that everything finally clicked!

She empowered and inspired me to go on a journey to self-discovery. I committed myself to the inner work that needed to take place regarding my money issues, self-worth, what I believed I deserved, what I was capable of, and why all of the things I was harbouring and dwelling on didn't matter. It was the very moment I DECIDED that I didn't need to accept life as a victim. I have the power within me to say/create how this thing gets to go.

Needless to say, clarity came quickly and EVERYTHING started to shift in a massive way.

I finally parted ways with the company.

A couple of months later, I closed on my very first home! I manifested every detail inside and out! The kids and I were thrilled! But I was still too scared to launch my personal brand, which led me back to the only income I knew best (MLM) with the thought process of 'this is my job'.

History of my success repeated itself and I reached founder within my first month and ranked up halfway through the comp plan in sixty days. I started to realise that the more I avoided the true calling of my life, the same obstacles kept recurring. I surrendered. I dealt with them head on and started planning for the incredible year. Tara Elle Inc. Business Empowerment and Success Coach was FINALLY open for business and it felt AMAZING! I launched my first group coaching program. It was a four-week intensive transformational mindset course that helped women to completely reprogram their subconscious mind and limiting beliefs into new beliefs, which then becomes their new physical reality that was intentionally designed.

On the day the cart closed, I generated 11k! That was an income amount that I hadn't seen in well over a year and it was in that moment that I knew I had finally found MY FOREVER HOME! It has been such a long journey with so many highs and lows but there was one thing that stayed the same; my passion to deeply support/transform women through a journey of wealth consciousness; along with a killer customised strategy. At Tara Elle Inc., I create a safe space for women where I fully support them and their desire to create a BIG EXPANSIVE life. I help them to drop their fear/ beliefs and fully step into their power and embody their highest self. They create a newfound confidence to show up in the world boldly shining their light. By them doing so, it creates a domino effect that inspires other women to do the same. They understand that being wildly successful and highly compensated is a byproduct of the amazing work they do in the world! A world where community, support and transformation is of top priority! Believe me when I say that Tara Elle Inc. is just getting started! The #ComebackQueens are about to disrupt the online space! The better it gets, the better it gets. Which means: the best is always yet to come! Stay tuned… XO

★★★

Tara's #1 passion in life besides being a mama to her two beautiful littles is pouring into other women and creating awareness around the importance of wealth mindset. After a long life of trial and error and many many struggles, she has finally blossomed into a super successful entrepreneur who is living out her dream life and business! She has dedicated her life to empowering women to pull their magic out and create a life they fully desire. One thing she knows for sure is that it doesn't matter where you've come from, where you are now, or what it looks like. All that matters is that you DECIDE. Decide that you are WORTHY of a big expansive life because: She who decides gets to have it all… and MORE! When she's not working she is either travelling the world with her babies, hanging with high level/ambitious gf's, spending time outside, or cooking up some yummy Italian food in the kitchen!

You can find Tara here:

Facebook.com/thetaraelleee

Instagram.com/taraelleee

How to Turn Your Pain into Your Superpower

Clare Reynolds

This book is dedicated to my closest friends who helped me through a really difficult time, Emma, Dani, Kelly, Alison, Mary, Jen and Jade. You each carried me when I wasn't able to carry myself. You showed me the true meaning of friendship and I will be eternally grateful.

To my Coach and Mentors, Liam, Lindsey Lewis and Denise, who have all contributed to my personal journey, showing me how to sit in my truth, becoming aligned with both my head and heart, not to mention supporting me to become an internationally accredited coach and NLP practitioner.

To Ryan who has supported me in Leaderships, showing me how I can positively make the world a better place. Teaching me how I can lead with love and purpose. You model the true essence of Leadership, showing me how I can always be better than yesterday.

To my family who have given me purpose and strength to always show up and keep going.

Finally to the woman who reads this who questions her self worth, her ability to love and lead. Who may be experiencing a challenging time in her life right now. I want nothing more than for you to find your inner warrior, harness the power of positive thinking and create a life beyond your wildest dreams because you are worthy and you always have a choice.

Toxic relationships can drain your energy and disconnect you from your truth.

Have you ever felt trapped in a relationship where you didn't feel loved, valued and appreciated? Where you felt pain from the very relationship that you once believed would bring you love and safety?

Can you visualise that moment?

Maybe you experienced feelings of loss, grief, anger, resentment, fear, or uncertainty? Can you recall how you responded and reacted to people, events and situations at that time around you, even the ones who really were only trying to help?

Did you ever say things you didn't mean in the heat of the moment because you were fueled by emotions of pain and anger? Perhaps you behaved out of character, responded to words and actions of others in a way that the version of you before that challenging time wouldn't normally react to?

I remember being in a difficult relationship where I felt like I tried desperately to fix it, to place all the focus on myself and place the responsibility to make it work all on me. I firmly believed that if I could change who I was it would all get better. I immersed myself in self-help books, implementing and testing theories I had come to learn, but to no avail. I then started to think it was me that was the problem. I mean, it had to be because I couldn't even get the ideas I read in a book to work.

Over time, the relationship disintegrated, to the point where we separated. I was always crying, surviving on little sleep, my head hurt and it felt like everything was wearing me down. At this point, I knew that mentally I was in a dangerous place. It was like quicksand. I would try hard to think positively but the negative thoughts just pulled me further and further down into a low mood, having panic attacks that caused so much pain right across my chest. I told myself in those moments that no one would actually care if I were here or not. Not many friends knew the extent as to how bad things really were; I tried hard to not be that friend that was so wrapped up in herself and her own problems.

There was one night where it all got so bad. In my head the negative thoughts wouldn't leave. I found myself unable to shift those thoughts of not wanting to be here anymore. I needed the noise in my head to just stop. I couldn't get out of my own head. I felt trapped in my own mind.

My friend and her family saved my life that night. It was one of the most incredible evenings I had had in a very long time. We laughed, we talked, we watched the stars and a meteor shower that happened. I felt a sense of belonging that night, finally. Love and laughter was

THE ELEVATION OF THE *Femalepreneur*

around me in abundance and it helped remove this dark heavy weight that was in my mind.

Back then, I really did feel like my life was over. The truth is my life had just begun.

Just before, I had started an online business. I was a busy mum juggling three children with a newborn baby, breastfeeding, a toddler and a soon-to-be teenager. All the responsibility of the house fell on my shoulders as well as going back to work five days a week during school hours. I then made a decision to go all in and handed my notice in at my job and within seventy-two hours I had replaced my monthly income.

When this relationship had ended it took me a little while but I was finally able to see it as an opportunity to go on a personal journey to heal within. When you are going through it, it doesn't make sense at the time, and that's okay, you aren't yet meant to know. You will come to know when the time is right. All I know now is that this breakup led to me experiencing personal growth on a whole new level. When I chose to take responsibility rather than place blame, I was able to acknowledge that I was the problem, my attitude and my mindset. Now I was finally sitting in my own truth.

Nothing that happened in my life was the fault of someone else.

Life happened FOR me not TO me.

But the greatest discovery of standing in my truth and recognising that I was the problem was that I learned I was also the solution.

So when the big stuff happens, because I have come to know more about who I really am and have the tools and techniques to shift my perspective and focus on gratitude, I could handle the big things better than I have ever done before.

During this healing journey, I let go of pain and resentment so that I could say to myself I will not allow another person to hold any space in my mind or spirit and I exercised this mental strength.

I cannot avoid pain, suffering or failures, they help shape the person I am.

But when these moments happen, I now no longer choose to live in that pain. I choose to move on.

I refuse to give up!

I use my mental resilience to keep pushing through what I thought was my limit.

I go to new levels, new heights, every time I do this consistently.

I have a choice!

I choose to take responsibility coupled with action every time.

My business skyrocketed as a result, I started to attract more people who were good for me and enhanced my life, and so many opportunities came my way that changed the trajectory of my life.

I chose to turn my pain into my superpower that helped me thrive through adversity as a woman in business and a mother. This was my time to have the most profound relationship in my entire life, one that focused deeply around unconditional love, acceptance and self-worth. It was the relationship with myself.

In the midst of what felt chaotic and like the end of my life, I came to realise that I was the person that had been missing from my life all along. I first had to be the one to take responsibility. It was no longer about right and wrong, good or bad, but what was more helpful. Self reflecting with openness and honesty for yourself takes real courage and I believe that this was one of the most enlightening moments of my healing journey that literally had my head and heart aligned, and it felt like a weight had been lifted.

A person is not their behaviour: something else I went on to learn and again this hit me really hard. To hear this, really hear this, it meant I had to change not only the way I saw other people, but also the way I saw myself too.

I honestly didn't know how to deal with this. It made me extremely uncomfortable. However, after the initial shock passed, I realised that it was more helpful for me to know this truth. To sit with it.

This is when I began to explore more in depth my thoughts with the help of my coach. I learned that whilst we cannot control another person's behaviour, we absolutely can and get to make a choice on how we react and respond to it.

In the past, if someone would do or say something, it would anger me, I would be so angry and upset and it would consume my day. I would react and respond with that emotion, which was not helpful for me. I felt I wouldn't be present as a mother, I would get distracted with work and miss showing up for things that were important or would push me forward. Instead I chose to stay in my story. To stay in victim mode.

It was what I was used to. It was what I had learned. It was easier to be there.

I never thought I would recover from self-doubt, lack of love and self-worth after being in a relationship like this. I thought that I would never trust someone again, never believe that I could have a fully functional relationship and I would never again have a feeling of hope or experience love. The woman I was before that relationship believed in happy ever afters where true love existed and these beliefs got destroyed by the end of this relationship.

As time moved on, I started to feel like I had fully recovered and healed but soon pieces of this relationship resurfaced again. During some NLP sessions, I recognised I had cut many cords that tied me to that relationship, but not all of them. There was still more work to do and at this point I felt deflated and frustrated with my personal growth. I felt like I was undoing all the progress I had made, but truly you can't undo any progress you make and this was a relief to learn.

Ultimately, I came to understand that I just wanted to feel heard. I needed someone to hold a space for me so that I could be vulnerable, and sit in my truth. There was a traumatised version of me that needed someone to listen in a way that was helpful. Someone who wouldn't give me advice or force their own beliefs and opinions on me and I found this person in my coach.

It was here that I had first-hand experience of the work a coach does. The ability they have to ask powerful, thought-provoking questions that no one else would typically ask me. It allowed me to have a far greater insight into myself. Seeing the results and positive changes this created in my own life, it spurred me on to become a coach myself. I went on to become a fully qualified and internationally accredited coach and an NLP practitioner. I never saw that coming. I believe that the experience I went through led me to be where I am now so that I can go on to help other men and women who are in a similar situation.

My mission as a coach is to not let people stay stuck in their stories. To guide them to have their own realisations. Helping them to see that they have choices in everything they do in life. That they do not need to surrender to the label of being a victim of their stories. More powerful than that, I want to help increase people's awareness around the notion that a person is not their behaviour because I found this lesson instrumental to my own recovery. To support others to heal and be able to enter into another relationship by trusting in their ability to make a decision that is right for them.

The work I now do with clients is one of the most rewarding outcomes to come from my own trauma. I lost a lot during the process; friends, beliefs and ways of doing things. However, I gained way more than I could have possibly imagined.

Internally, I increased my self-worth, self-love, confidence and the value I saw in myself. I significantly increased my ability to be present as a mother with my children. I found the courage to enter into a new relationship and trust in my new abilities to do what is right for me.

I later went on to speak on stage, find a whole community of like-minded people, and be given more opportunities to speak on stage and share my story where I help change other people's lives. Fifteen months down the line and I am unstoppable. Every day I use this experience, the pain, to propel me forward in all areas of my life.

I am by no means a finished article. Self-development and healing is a journey. But I am definitely where I am meant to be, doing the things I am meant to do.

Remember, your thoughts determine your feelings, which determine the action you take and the outcome you have.

If you take anything from this chapter, please write that down, it is your new superpower to get back up from any challenging time in your life. With this tool you can go on to find your inner warrior, harness the power of positive thinking and create a life beyond your wildest dreams.

★★★

Clare Reynolds helps online coaches leverage more time with online digital and tech support. She is described as an incredible coach and an expert within her field.

Clare is very passionate about using her story to inspire other women who may have been through similar situations to her and she believes we all have the power within us to heal and create the success we desire.

Clare loves spending time with her friends and family when she isn't working and when she is working, she never fails to inspire and empower others with her strength.

You can find Clare here:

https://clarereynoldsva.co.uk/
https://www.facebook.com/clarereynolds86/
https://www.instagram.com/clarereynolds86/

YOU ARE THE CREATOR – THE POWER LIES WITHIN YOU!

Natasha Edwards

This chapter is dedicated to all of my fellow femalepreneurs out there who are building their empires.

I want you to know that it doesn't matter what your past is, what failures you've had previously, what adversity or struggles you've had to face along your journey. No matter how hard things may seem, NEVER give up on your dreams.

As I opened my eyes in a dark strange place, my thoughts took over… where am I, how did I get here, is this heaven or am I still stuck in hell?

Then the pain hit me. I felt sick from all of the drugs swirling around in my system, my wrist was throbbing from where I had cut it, my heart hurt because it had been shattered into a thousand pieces and I felt that same sunken feeling of depression that had become the only emotion I'd grown to know!

Then came the huge wave of anxiety that completely took over my mind, body and soul, panic swirled inside… what am I going to do with my life, how am I going to cope on my own, I can't be a single mum when I still felt like a child myself. The panic and overwhelming thoughts took my breath away and made my heart feel like it was going to jump out of my chest!

I wasn't meant to wake up, WHY was I still being forced to live in the hellhole my life had become?!

I didn't have any strength left in me because the ten-year drug-fuelled volatile relationship I had just been through had stripped every bit of strength and dignity I had left!

It had stripped me of my self-worth, of my identity, of my character and had made me into someone I barely recognised.

The confident party girl I had been in my teens was now a shy, paranoid, hurt little girl who didn't trust a soul in this world because everyone she thought she could trust had betrayed her or let her down.

Here I was once again at rock bottom and needing to rebuild my life, but this time I had no strength to do it, I literally just wanted to die!

The drugs, violence, crime, cheating, betrayal, lies and the narcissistic mental abuse I had to go through day in day out for the last ten years had killed me as an individual and I didn't even know where to start with piecing myself back together again.

The pain of my reality and the lost soul I had become was far too much to cope with and to me the only way out was to take my own life.

As I lay there sobbing into my pillow, I knew I had two options.

Go back there, continue living in the drug hell my life had become and soon enough I'd die, exiting this world without ever leaving my mark on it.

Or get out, find my strength, heal and create the life I'd always known I was brought here to live!

You see, I'd always had this knowing, even through my darkest of times. I had this vision that had followed me around from as far back as I can remember.

I was on stage, speaking, empowering and having an impact on others.

It made no sense to me what it was because at the time my life was a mess and I was far from feeling empowered myself, but I knew it was my intuition and my soul telling me there was another life out there for me, once I finally found the courage to leave the one I thought I was trapped in behind!

I had always been intuitive, ever since I was a little girl. I'd known there was another world outside of the physical one that we live in, but I'd never fully understood it until recently.

But as I grew, that vision of being on stage never left my side and here I was at my lowest point, after trying to take my own life and it was coming into my head yet again!

I knew it was the universe telling me to get out of this relationship because there was a new life waiting for me outside of it.

It was time to get my life on track and be the mummy my boy deserved.

So I threw myself into single mum life, doing the

best I could to get by, but I was so unhappy, carrying all of this guilt and shame and hurt from my past; I was walking around broken with an empty smile.

As I muddled through every day, lost, lonely and depressed, I'd wonder when I'd finally find the path I was meant to be on.

I had a job as a stylist in a busy salon, just about getting by as a single mum, but I still knew deep inside that I was brought here to do so much more with my life, yet the question was, what?!

Then one day out of the blue, my friend came knocking at my door.

She presented me with an opportunity.

I didn't believe it was real, so I hesitated for six months, watching her drastically change her life whilst mine remained the same.

Then eventually, I decided to go for it, my intuition and gut feeling was too strong not to and that vision of being on stage was popping up more than ever!

A whisper within said, 'This is the opportunity that's about to change your life,' so I knew I had to act on it and let my soul lead the way.

Little old me was starting a business… who would have thought it? I was about to start my entrepreneurial journey.

I felt all kinds of emotions, happy, excited, nervous, worried if I was good enough to make it work, scared in case I wasn't doing the right thing, but I knew I had to push through the fear and just do it, because staying in my comfort zone stuck behind the salon chair wasn't getting me anywhere!

So, I went all in!

I absorbed every bit of information I could, took on board what I was being told to do and took ten times the action I needed to.

I pushed through my family laughing at me.

I stayed up late and woke up early to work on my business before I went to work.

I became a sponge and soaked up all of the skills and training I needed.

And most importantly, I actioned it, making mistakes and learning lessons along the way!

I found this was giving me a focus.

It had introduced myself to personal development, mindset and spirituality; I was loving soaking up the positivity and becoming a new me!

I felt like a new woman.

I woke up refreshed and energised and feeling naturally high on life, no drugs or alcohol needed, I was vibing high!

My business was growing.

I was committed!

Instead of partying, I'd attend success seminars, and suddenly my vision was making sense. I could finally see how I would be up there too, how I would be walking the stage!

I started learning about the law of attraction, I had my eye on a certain position within my business and I wanted to see if this manifesting thing was real!

Like I mentioned earlier, I'd always had this knowing that another world existed outside of this physical one we live in and my intuition had never let me down throughout my life. I knew I had to trust what I was being drawn to!

This is when I was introduced to abundance cheques and I'll never forget the first one I wrote.

If you don't know what they are, it's when you ask the universe for what you want, you write it down and set the intention and then keep a positive outlook on that goal happening in your physical reality whilst taking action towards making it happen.

I wrote down that I wanted to earn £1000 from my business.

This was a huge goal to me, especially seeing as I'd only started it twelve weeks beforehand!

But I was determined, and I wanted to see if this LOA stuff was real!

I mean, I was feeling and looking the best I had in a long time from following it, but could I actually create the life I wanted, was I in control of my life, did my thoughts actually create my reality?

Let's put this thing to the damn test!

So, I wrote the cheque and dated it 30th November 2014.

Then I went all in, I visualised it happening every day, I felt the feeling of having it NOW, I believed it was on its way with no doubt at all and I took massive action to make it happen!

The end of the month came and my business paycheque arrived in my email.

I was due to be paid over £900, HOLY FUCK!

It was real, I did it, I could change my life through my way of thinking!

I will never forget the excitement I felt.

I soon became obsessed with the LOA and my spiritual journey and evolvement began.

Being connected, awakened and activated was the BEST feeling ever!

I wrote another cheque for the pivotal position I'd been striving for in my business.

Hands shaking, I wrote down the huge goal to be manager March 31st 2015. Now this was a HUGE goal because in reality and on paper there was no way I could achieve it in three and a half weeks with how my business looked, but with my gut feeling and new found belief, I got to work and went for it like my life depended on it!

I will never forget walking through my parents' door at the end of the day on 31st of March 2015, sinking onto the sofa and sobbing. I'd done it, little old me had done it and on the exact date I'd set the intention to do it too!

I'd hit manager. God knows how I'd made it happen, but I did, and I knew in that moment that deep inside of me there was this power far greater than me controlling the whole thing. I knew that if I just stayed tapped into this power and followed my intuition then whatever I wanted would come my way!

That's the moment I realised the power of the universe. That's the moment I knew this knowing I'd had since I was a little girl was real. That's the moment I thought OMG the power to create the life I wanted really did lie in my hands!

Things progressed well and quickly, I got my new house, my new Audi, I left my job and life was amazing!

My spiritual evolvement continued, as did the ups and downs of my entrepreneurial journey.

I was starting to feel more pulled towards coaching others to success.

One day, during a meditation, I had a vision come to me.

To start an academy, teaching network marketers all of these online business tools I had recently learned that had brought me and my clients lots of success.

I intuitively downloaded the information I was being told and the strategy in what to do. I could see it clearly, but I could feel that I wasn't going to do it alone.

I brainstormed for days, planning everything out, the excitement too much to handle!

I kept feeling drawn to ask a then client of mine (Jo, who's in the next chapter) if she wanted to join forces and open the academy with me.

She had a similar background to me, and we were so similar in many ways, I knew we would work well together.

She would cover mindset and I would teach the business strategy.

I knew both were needed as they played such an important part in the journey of an entrepreneur!

Excitedly, we got to work, we planned it carefully, took massive inspired action and worked our butts off.

The whole time we were in complete flow with

the universe. The alignment and energy of it all felt incredible and we had the perfect success strategy to follow, as I'd just invested to learn it!

Within six weeks we had built it from nothing to a whopping 70k turnover and thousands of followers!

We couldn't believe what we had just achieved – once again I had my intuition and the higher power to thank for leading me in this direction!

Since launching Femalepreneurs Academy, it's been a crazy whirlwind of ups and downs but the main thing I've learned along the way over the last six years of being on this journey is that we can do anything when we are connected and in trust with the universe as we are fully in our femalepreneur power.

The minute we are disconnected we lose our power and start to live in fear, which then causes abundance blocks and lack of success.

One of my favourite quotes is, "It's not what you do it's who you are in the process."

In our academy we teach a mixture of strategy and soul for a reason; strategy is important but it's that spiritual connection you have with the divine that really makes all of the difference to your business success.

When you have this, magic happens, your intuition is strong, and you are divinely guided in the direction of unstoppable success. You are able to choose faith over fear and miracles happen – miracles like I've told in this story.

The impossible becomes possible!

There is nothing special about me, I don't hold a

secret key to success. If I can go from where I came from to where I am now, then so can you!

I've just learned that the power lies within me and I let my soul lead the way and, in doing so, the success follows.

I'm an elevated femalepreneur and just a girl who decided to go for it, stay connected, trust instead of fear. You are stronger and more capable than you think. Everything you've ever wanted is out there and available to you when you elevate, connect, trust and go for it – always let your soul lead the way because it already knows your destiny.

You've got this, femalepreneur. Stop worrying over things that haven't yet happened because everything is working out perfectly for you, just how it should be. No matter how hard things may seem, they may even feel like they are falling apart, trust that we've got your back and when eventually things fall into place you'll see why they went the way they did and you wouldn't have it any other way.

You can't connect the dots looking forward, you can only connect them looking backwards. Trust, my dear, that the universe has your back and that things are always working out for you.

Now go out there and enjoy every moment of your journey because, at the end of it, all you'll have are the memories – it's your duty to make sure they're good ones.

★★★

Natasha is a single mum, entrepreneur and life success influencer. She helps ambitious women discover the benefits of working online to live their ideal life. She teaches a combination of mindset, law of attraction and business strategy. Her passion is to help Femalepreneurs find a way to do business that feels good to them and to encourage ambitious women to start their entrepreneurial journey and create a life beyond their wildest of dreams.

You can find Natasha here:

https://www.facebook.com/xxtashaa

BELIEVE YOU CAN AND YOU'RE HALFWAY THERE! NEVER GIVE UP!

JoJo Ellen

I dedicate this chapter to every single person in my life who ever told me I couldn't do something, ever doubted me and ever inflicted any pain or trauma onto me. Because of you, I am a success and I love the woman I have become! You are the reason I kept going no matter what.

I dedicate this to Tomáš, the love of my life – for always giving me the strength to keep going and always believing in me even when I never did.

I dedicate this to my family – for raising me and always making sure I was safe, loved and an honourable, respectable woman.

And all my fellow femalepreneurs working hard to achieve your dreams – keep crushing, ladies, you've got this!

For so long I always had a dream of making something of myself, I just didn't know what it was. I grew up with a great family around me who always wanted the best for me.

I always remember throughout my childhood not

understanding a lot and being easily confused by things at school. I think I was just a slow learner and I definitely lacked confidence as a kid! I was bullied and belittled pretty much in every single year of my school life by multiple different people. I was the black sheep, the odd one out and, wherever I went, I found it really hard to fit in. My school years were hard because of my lack of confidence, my lack of understanding for things and the bullying all together. Even though I had wonderful friends and knew great people, it actually caused me not to try hard at anything whatsoever because I just didn't see the point. I used to say to myself in my own head 'well what's the point? I'm only going to fail anyway, no one will care'.

As time went on from this point, my parents started their own business running a pub and we had to move away from all my childhood friends, which I found hard at first, but soon got used to it.

School continued, and so did the bullying. Bullies at school started a rumour that I lied about moving house to try and 'be cool' because I was living in a pub. A few years later, it got so bad I had to leave school early before lunchtime and go out of a back entrance so no one would wait for me to attack me. I would meet my mum there and she would take me home to continue schooling me for the rest of the day. This went on for my final years of school and I failed all my GCSEs.

Fast forward a few years, and I was a rebellious teenager drinking, smoking and staying out at all hours with friends, dating guys who were not right for me at all. I ended up being in numerous emotionally and physically abusive relationships.

I was so used to be being beaten down mentally and physically that I just took it from everyone I met. At this point, I was a very, very broken young girl with absolutely no hope and no clue.

Fast forward to eighteen, I decided to embark on a new journey into education. I went and studied media studies, journalism, writing and film creation and editing. I did this for two years and landed a distinction in every area, top of my class. I also bagged myself a job at a music venue, which I loved and was living in a shared house with friends.

Finally, life was good, or so I'd hoped – a job, qualifications and independence but, along the way, there were more challenging relationships (to say the least) and I ended up having what felt like a breakdown. I hit the bottle. I was drinking every single day, going out every single Friday, Saturday and Sunday night with different groups of friends and, by this point, I'd become bar manager of the music venue, gained more qualifications in beauty therapy, which I did absolutely nothing with, and I was barely able to afford to keep the roof over my head and eat.

The drinking got worse and I met a few people who I started hanging out with more and more. As my life was spiralling further and further down, I found something that I thought would pick me up – and it was drugs. Class A's to be more, well… specific. Everyone was doing it, I thought. So why not? I had nothing better to do.

Before I knew it, I was out every night of the week after my job finished at the music venue but this time I wasn't just drinking. I was partying it up and hard!

I came to a point shortly after this and just thought to myself: what the actual fuck am I doing with my life?

So again, here I was – lost, depressed and stuck in a rut with absolutely no idea what to do with my life. I didn't have many friends at this time – only friends that wanted to party – which I still did continue to see, but I knew deep down what I was doing to myself was wrong and I needed to stop. I just didn't know how.

I remember waking up one day, completely out of the blue, and I just felt different. By this time, I was around twenty-one or twenty-two years old, still working at the music venue and I felt the sudden urge to hand in my notice. I had no idea why I felt the way that I did that day, but all I knew is that I wanted out. I was done. I was ready to pack my old life up and leave it behind.

After this period of my life, I had settled into a new job working as a carer for vulnerable adults and I loved it. I loved my colleagues and I loved the nature of my job because I have always been a very caring person. I learned so many incredible things working there. I really grew as a person and for that I will always be so grateful.

During this time, after receiving my beauty therapy qualifications, I had a few nail clients on the side to earn extra money. One day I had a new client book in with me and I went to her house really excited. I've always been in tune with my intuition but never understood it back then. I just felt this unwavering feeling and it felt good! I felt as if something incredible was going to happen.

Was I right? Yes, I was! I was offered a network marketing opportunity and I signed up there and then.

I was sceptical at first because of the typical things everyone says: 'it's a pyramid scheme; no one ever earns money with those things; you are joining a cult', etc., etc. Bear in mind, even though I was working a new job, I still had debts under my belt from previous times when I could barely afford to keep a roof over my head. My partying days saw me with payday loans, credit cards and the longest 'I O U' list known to man, so as you can imagine, I needed all the money I could get!

So, I said yes and that was it. My network marketing business was born and I absolutely loved it. The products, the concept, the people I had met were incredible and my eyes were opened to the amazing possibilities of work from home opportunities and what they can give you.

I worked within my care job for the next four to five years whilst building my business online. By this point, I was earning more than an average full-time wage with my business on top of my actual full-time wage. I loved having the extra finances and was able to live extremely comfortably and I also became debt free thanks to this incredible industry! Throughout this time, I had been with a few different network marketing companies because I never really felt as if I found my fit. As usual, the black sheep, the weirdo, the outcast.

As time went on, even though I was earning an insane amount of money every month, close to five figures, I started losing my passion for the industry. Again, I always knew I was meant for more in this life, I just didn't know what. When I joined the industry, I really thought 'this is it. This is what I'm meant for', but I just couldn't put my finger on what the problem was.

Throughout the years of me being in the industry, I learned all about personal development and mindset growth and I really started growing and developing my inner spirit too. I found the law of attraction, and started practising meditation. I developed a real strong sense of my own intuition and started learning all about alignment.

And that's when I realised what the problem was. I wasn't aligned to this line of work any more. So many ups and downs had occurred within my journey, I met some lovely people, but jeez did I meet some God-awful ones as well. I was deceived, lied to, used, but also met friends for life, changed my life completely from a financial and personal growth perspective and had some really fun times that I never would have been able to have if it were not for the network marketing industry.

So, I really felt like at that time, it was no longer for me.

I started diving more into my personal development and thought what else could I do aside from network marketing to make an income? So, I was researching online one day and found a life coaching course, which I paid for and then became certified. I also found a marketing coach shortly afterward, who I hired to teach me how to have marketing in place to generate leads, have an online system and regular paying clients every month.

I really wanted to give this a go, so I put my all into it and, in the first month of coaching, I made my investment back and then some! I made a very healthy four-figure sum, which got me excited and made me realise the potential of the online coaching space. I pursued it more and then that coach actually asked me to go into business with her, so I did, and The Femalepreneurs Academy was born.

Now, you've just heard from Natasha in the previous chapter and, as you'd have read, she also has a very crazy past, so we related on many, many levels. I thought she'd be the perfect business partner, as we had both had struggles, overcame them, but also success in the same industry – network marketing!

Now, my journey and transition into coaching was not a swift one by any means. I have been ridiculed, trolled to the nines, sent death threats within the last twelve months, had people try and close my Facebook account for no reason, and had people try to continuously sabotage my business.

It's HARD, guys. I am telling you. Now, I am not going to sit here and say I have been an innocent party in my journey. I have made a tonne of mistakes along the way. I have ruffled feathers, I have pissed people off, I have said all the wrong things, I have gossiped, and whatever else... Let's be real here, who hasn't?! But I had to go on that self-discovery and challenging journey within myself to learn the hard way, and I know for a fact I have come out of the other side.

I know how hard it is to grow a business in a world where you're misunderstood, feel as if you're not liked for always being true to yourself and honest, or have people be so jealous of you and your success that they start rumours and try to tear down everything you've ever worked for.

The highs and lows of entrepreneurship are real. It's not easy but is it worth it? Heck yeah, it's worth it!

Something else I recently achieved is I became a certified practitioner in NLP, Timeline Therapy™ and hypnotherapy, which has enabled me to release a lot of negative emotions I used to feel, and let go of so much of my past and just forgive. I let go of the pain I have held onto for so long, I let go of the anger I had for all those people in my life and finally set my soul free. I no longer live in resentment and guilt; I no longer have this disbelief within myself of 'I'm not good enough' or 'no-one will take me seriously'. I have achieved so much in my life and I have forgiven every single person who ever treated me badly, betrayed and abused me, bullied and traumatised me, every single person who said I wouldn't achieve, and of course those who have been there for me too.

My life sure has been a roller coaster of a journey, but do you know what? I have conquered many a battle. A battle of alcoholism, drug abuse, being abused – emotionally, physically, you name it – I have overcome and also grown from it. I haven't touched a single drug in over three years and never will again, and I only drink now when I celebrate – I'm not that lost little girl any more. I found her, I looked after her and I guided her through every single dark time she ever had.

I never let people get me down, not for too long anyway. I always got back up when times got hard, I never listened to a single thing that those bullies told me and I always used every single negative experience to drive me forward because, if I didn't, who knows where I would be today?

My life has come a long, long way since those times and I hope that anybody reading this has found courage and strength to get up and keep going too. To go from a broke, lost, abused girl, to a strong, empowered, successful businesswoman and number one bestselling author – if I can overcome it, you sure as heck can too. I always look back and smile and imagine that poor, young, vulnerable lost girl and I keep her with me every single day within my soul. I always say, 'You've got this, girl. Be proud of your incredible journey so far, and love the strong, wise woman you have become.'

We all deserve our dreams and have the capabilities within ourselves to achieve it. It just starts with believing it first. The rest will follow, just trust you and always trust the process!

★★★

Jo is used to referring to herself as a very misunderstood character. For so many years, she's struggled to find where she belongs. She has always been true to herself and shone her light onto those around her, even those who may have mistreated her. She sees the best in everybody and in every situation and is a very kind-hearted soul. She now doesn't refer to herself as that misunderstood girl she once thought she was. She also doesn't feel like she no longer belongs… She has paved the way for herself and others like her and now embraces her own light and inspires many others to embrace themselves too.

Jo is a professional network marketer, a mindset, business and social media marketing coach and an author. She believes in equality, always being true to yourself and it's her mission to inspire fellow women all around the globe.

You can find JoJo here:

www.facebook.com/JoJoxEllen

SUMMARY

You see? You really can get through the tough times. Every single curveball thrown at us femalepreneurs, however big or small, we got through it and still kept chasing our dreams. We had a choice. To either give up on everything and let our past, our scars, whether physical or emotional, define us and hold us back forever or we could stand back up after every hit and come back that little bit stronger every single time!

We will keep rising from the darkness and allow our lights to shine through and be a beacon of hope to anyone out there who truly needs it.

So, if like any of us, there's been pain, hurt, trauma and fears, find the courage from within to push through it and be the femalepreneur you were destined to be! Your future self will thank you for it!

This is *The Elevation of The Femalepreneur*, and we will continue to rise together!

You can find The Femalepreneurs Academy here:
www.femalepreneursacademy.com
Membership: http://bit.ly/InfluenceandImpactAcademy
Facebook group: https://www.facebook.com/
groups/1225161520949628/